BORN TO PREACH

Official Biography of

DR. A. E. PRINCE

BY CARVIN C. BRYANT
Pastor Maplewood Park Baptist Church
President Illinois Baptist State Association

HERALD PRINTING COMPANY
Collinsville, Illinois

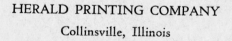

TO
DR. W. P. THROGMORTON

FOUNDER OF THE
ILLINOIS BAPTIST STATE ASSOCIATION

FIRST EDITOR OF THE ILLINOIS BAPTIST

DEFENDER OF THE FAITH
IN FIFTY RELIGIOUS DEBATES

GREAT-HEARTED PASTOR AND
DENOMINATIONAL LEADER WHO SPENT MOST OF
HIS LONG LIFE AMONG THE PEOPLE
OF SOUTHERN ILLINOIS

GREAT IN STATURE, IN WORD, AND IN DEED
AMONG WHOSE MONUMENTS ARE THE BEAUTIFUL
HOUSE OF WORSHIP OF MARION FIRST CHURCH,
THE ILLINOIS BAPTIST, AND THE
ILLINOIS BAPTIST STATE ASSOCIATION

A MAN OF CRYSTAL CHARACTER,
AND DEDICATED LEADERSHIP

AND TO ALL WHO JOINED WITH HIM
IN THE FOUNDING OF THE
ILLINOIS BAPTIST STATE ASSOCIATION

THIS BOOK IS AFFECTIONATELY DEDICATED

As some tall cliff that lifts its awful form
Breaks from the vale and midway leaves the storm
Though round its breast the rolling clouds are spread
Eternal sunshine settles on its head.

Biography is a feeble struggle with death. It is an attempt to retain something of the man, his spirit and manner of thinking and feeling, that he being dead may yet speak.

TABLE OF CONTENTS

TABLE OF CONTENTS (Continued)

ILLUSTRATIONS

FOREWORD

When I came to the pastorate of Maplewood Park Baptist Church, I was impressed with my predecessor's keen insight to spiritual things. He had no axes to grind and he spoke ill of no person. He went about his work with grace and dignity.

In the life of Dr. A. E. Prince is being fulfilled Robert Browning's prophecy as voiced by Rabbi Ben Ezra in these inspiring words:

> Grow old along with me!
> The best is yet to be,
> The last of life, for which the first was made:
> Our times are in His hand
> Who saith "A whole I planned,
> Youth shows but half; trust God: see all
> nor be afraid!

The likes of this eighty-year-old minister is not apt to reappear. For this reason I wanted to share with the future generations the experience and challenge of meeting him.

Having known Dr. Prince for many years prior to the present time, I felt that a biography of him would make an invaluable contribution to our generation. When I first approached him about writing it, he chuckled in "Prince style" and said, ' There isn't anything to write." And he was not just being modest. He actually thought he was right. After I had talked with him of its possibilities and allowed him to think about it for some time, he consented to let me start and see what could be done. He wrote me this note:

"AIN'T WE GOT FUN?"

> My pastor, blessings on him, has it in his heart to write a history of my life, a biography, "er sumthin." What a shock is ahead for him! This has never been undertaken before, because there is nothing to write. Lord Byron said it for me, when he wrote: "My ancient but ignoble blood, has flown through scoundrels ever since the flood." In a moment of weakness, I agreed to be the victim of his epistolary ambitions, and so here goes. May a gracious Providence sustain both of us in this slippery ordeal! "Ain't we got fun?"

Keeping him still long enough to get the information was no small chore. Eighty years have not slowed him to any noticeable degree. He does as much as any young pastor with whom I am acquainted. He has had two jobs most of his life. At present, he is serving as full-time pastor and as an executive administrator for a development in St. Louis. He has kept good records through the years—even has the outline of his first sermon, which he consented for me to use. He was most generous in opening his files and providing me with much of the needed data. Also, he has been generous with his time. It has been an enriching experience to sit with him and talk of his sixty-four years in the active ministry and of his childhood days. His mind is as alert and disciplined as that of any person I have ever met.

When I accepted the Maplewood Park pastorate, I assured Dr. and Mrs. Prince that I would be delighted for them to retain their church membership at Maplewood. They said they would be happy to do this for awhile and see how it worked out. However, they stated that if any problem arose, they would transfer to another church at a time when it could be done gracefully in order not to create any problems for me.

We agreed that I would be his pastor and he would be my pastor, and we would "pasteurize each other!" We have had many wonderful hours together. I feel I am better by having had this close relationship with him and wiser by having had the privilege of working with him. He called me his only sheep until I got him entangled with this book. But lately when I call him, he says "Oh, this is my goat."

Preaching is his business; the pulpit is his throne. He is often called the dean of ministers of the Illinois Baptist State Association, a title well earned by his sixty-four years in the Baptist ministry and his assistance in organizing the Illinois Baptist State Association in 1907.

In our move to Maplewood Park an accident occured which hospitalized Mrs. Bryant and me. One of the first faces I remember seeing in the hospital was that of Dr. Prince, who had continued serving the church until I arrived. The future for me was questionable for a few hours, and I asked Dr. Prince to take care of the church until I recovered. He carried on the work of the church for three more months in a very fine way.

My hope for this volume is that it will find its way into the hands of young people. I believe it will challenge them to become partners with God as they begin their pilgrimage into the future.

Gratitude must be expressed to our two church secretaries, Mrs. Betty Laxton and Mrs. Jeannette Parker, for their faithful service in typing, retyping, and retyping the manuscript, and to Mrs. V. A. Fielden and to Mrs. Ruth McCuistion for painstaking work in typing copy for the book, and to Rev. George Tourney, Pastor Winstanley Baptist Church, East St. Louis, for designing the jacket. I am also indebted to Dr. Prince's daughter, Mrs. Edwin F. Moore, Professor of English, Baylor University, for invaluable help in reviewing and correcting the manuscript and for helpful suggestions about the work; and to Mrs. A. E. Prince, who is Dr. Prince's helper in all things, for many helpful suggestions about the preparation and publication of the book, and for her contagious interest and joy in the progress of this venture.

Great care has been exercised to give proper acknowledgement for any copyrighted material used in this book. We are deeply grateful to the Baptist Sunday School Board for permission to quote from several of B. B. McKinney's hymns on which they hold copyright. We will appreciate any information concerning any other copyrighted material, if any, inadvertantly used and will make due acknowledgements in event any mistake has been made in this matter.

More than one year of time has been given to the preparation of this book, with several working at the task as they could find the time. The burden of the prayer of these workers has been that in spite of any mistakes occuring from human weakness, the book may have the blessing of God upon it as it passes from our hands to the hands of many readers. May God add His blessing to our efforts to portray the life of one distinguished servant of our Lord and Master.

Carvin C. Bryant, Pastor
Maplewood Park Baptist Church
President Illinois Baptist State Association

June 1, 1967

I.

LIFE OF DR. PRINCE IN BRIEF

Jesus Christ was born in the little village of Bethlehem, whose chief claim to immortality in history is the fact of His birth. Abraham Lincoln was born in a log cabin in an obscure community in Kentucky. It is impossible to foretell who will be renowned or remain obscure by merely assessing his birthplace. Some who attain greatness may come from the great city, but it is just as likely that some rural place will be the birthplace of a person destined to be renowned.

It was in an obscure place that Aaron Erastus Prince was born—Lamard Township, Wayne County, Illinois—on January 1, 1887, the first child of Rev. and Mrs. Peter Prince. Providence so ordered it that he was not born in a palace, but in a one-room log school-house which was located near old Victory Church and cemetery, and which was the home of his parents at that time. He regards the place of his birth as singular, for the old log school-house furnished the intellectual setting for this event, the church furnished a religious background, and the cemetery furnished the sombre state of mind which has continued throughout his life to remind him that the spirit of mortals should never be proud. All of these things have cast their influence over his life, and have contributed so much to him that he avers that he cannot lay claim to the political gimmick that he is a self-made man.

His maternal grandparents were Rev. and Mrs. Cephas Adolphus Young. His grandfather Young was an outstanding preacher in Southern Illinois for a generation. Their daughter, Emma Jane Young, had grown to womanhood in the Victory Church Community. His father, Rev. Peter Prince, son of Mr. and Mrs. William Ivans Prince, was born near Thackery in Hamilton County, Illinois, and was one of the leading preachers of Southern Illinois for forty-two years. There is a long line of preachers in the ancestry of Dr. Prince. He feels that foreordination, working through ancestry, contrived to

His father's old pulpit

put him into the ministry. But one of his favorite Scriptures is, "And I thank Christ Jesus our Lord, who hath enabled me . . . . putting me into the ministry . . . . And the grace of our Lord was exceeding abundant with faith and love which is in Christ Jesus." (I Timothy 1:12, 14). The reader will find many interesting things in the following pages about his childhood days, and other events of his long and useful life of service for the Lord.

He grew up on a farm and spent many hours alone with God in the fields. He was converted in a revival in a small village church and has the old pulpit behind which his father stood and preached at that service. He dedicated his life to God out in the open field and was called to preach as he prayed alone in the field.

His ministry has been evangelistic. He has held many revivals in churches, small and large, over a wide area. Some have been in St. Louis and Kansas City, Missouri; Denver, Colorado; San Diego, California; Shreveport, Baton Rouge, Lake Charles and New Orleans, Louisiana; Little Rock, Elaine, Texarkana and Arkadelphia, Arkansas; Newport and Hopkinsville, Kentucky; Atlanta and Augusta, Georgia; Oxford, North Carolina; Charleston, South Carolina; Miami, Florida; Roswell, New Mexico; San Antonio, Cisco and Fort Worth, Texas; Burlington, Iowa; Broken Bow, Nebraska; Parsons, Kansas; Parsons, Tennessee; Phoenix City, Alabama; Honolulu, Hawaii, and in yet other places. He has held three or four revivals in some of these cities, and has held most of the revivals in his own churches through the years.

He has been pastor in five states; district missionary, foreign missionary, stewardship evangelist, soul-winning evangelist; author, editor; three times a college president, principal of one academy, director of two financial campaigns which saved two colleges from bankruptcy; chaplain of a U.S. Veteran's Hospital, a State Hospital, a State Industrial School for girls, and a Baptist hospital; and administrator and chaplain of a Retirement Home. He says that he is still looking for more worlds to conquer.

In addition to his work as pastor-evangelist, missionary,

educator, author, chaplain, administrator, financier, world traveler and editor, he has been a family man and maintained a Christian home for the six children which God gave to him and his first wife. The children are all Christians, all were baptized by their father, five of them married by their father (one is not married), and all of them in honorable positions, and distinguished in their professions, and in their churches. He now lives in the first home he has ever owned with his second wife, to whom he was married three years after his first wife passed away. They call their home "*Dun Travelyn*" and hope they are through moving at last.

He has consented to the release of this book, not for publicity or praise for himself, but rather that young people who read the book may be inspired to make the most of life. He feels that he will be amply repaid for the release of the book if the Lord will use this book to inspire some young person to dedicate his life to God. One of the convictions of his life is that the world has yet to see what God can do with one fully dedicated man. Here at the beginning of the book I am listing some of the highpoints of his ministry.

1. Supplying the pulpits of Dr. George W. Truett, Dr. Marshall Craig, Dr. T. A. Patterson, Dr. M. E. Dodd, Dr. Guy Moore, Dr. Millard Jenkins, and other great ministers of great churches.
2. The unusual privilege of performing the marriage ceremony for his widowed mother in 1919.
3. Declined the election to the office of State Sunday School Secretary of Illinois in 1920.
4. A most unusual funeral service in Pineville in 1935.
5. Preaching in John Jasper's famous church in Richmond, Virginia, at the Sunday morning service when the Southern Baptist Convention met in that city in 1938.
6. A number of great revivals in which more than one hundred people were won to Christ. In two of these—at Pineville, Louisiana and Arkadelphia, Arkansas—perhaps as many as five hundred marked definite decisions for

Christ in their lives.

7. His work as president of three colleges and one academy, and especially his success in saving his Alma Mater to the Baptists of Missouri.
8. His address to an audience of five thousand, without benefit of a public address system, at the dedication of the monument which marks the spot of the famous Lincoln-Douglas debate at Charleston, Illinois.
9. His baccalaureate sermons and graduating class addresses in many schools, the most outstanding of these being his baccalaureate sermons at John Tarleton College in Texas, and at Southern Illinois University.
10. His work in New Zealand and Hawaii. He has the distinction of being the only Southern Baptist preacher ever to serve as pastor of a New Zealand Church—the historic Baptist Tabernacle, Auckland, New Zealand. He had the honor of preaching the Convention sermon on Sunday at the annual meeting of the New Zealand Baptist Assembly in the Capital City of Wellington in 1951. In Hawaii, he organized a church and founded a liberal arts college.
11. His painstaking work for his beloved denomination, including serving on three Southwide Boards—Education, Foreign Mission and Annuity Boards—and on a number of important Southwide Committees.
    —Member of the State Board in three states.
    —District Missionary and Foreign Missionary.
    —Author of seven books.
    —Listed in **Who's Who in America** for the past twenty-five years, and in twelve other national and international biographical books.
    —Alternate preacher, annual sermon, Southern Baptist Convention, Atlanta, Georgia, 1924.
    —Pastor of hundreds of young ministers, scores of these ordained by him for life service as ministers and missionaries.
    —Officiated at hundreds of funerals and weddings.
    —One of two living survivors of the founders of the Illinois Baptist State Association in 1907;* Member and Recording Secretary of the Board of Directors for years; President Board of Trustees, Ewing College, for years, and the last president of the college; saw Baptist

* According to L. H. Moore's history, "Southern Baptists in Illinois," J. B. Kelly and A. E. Prince are the only survivors of the founders of the Illinois Baptist State Association. Brother Kelly, 92 years young, lives at Johnston City, Illinois.

Children's Home grow from a farm with one tent on it to the present plant, and the State Association grow from a small group of churches in Southern Illinois to almost 1,000 churches today spread all over Illinois.

—Outstandingly successful pastorates in a number of large churches in which he has served in five states and one foreign country, climaxing with what he calls his "Golden Pastorate" at Maplewood Park Baptist Church.

—He is a graduate of three schools of higher education, has seven years of theological training, and two of the colleges from which he was graduated, have conferred on him the honorary doctorate. He was the youngest man ever to receive the Doctor of Divinity Degree from Ewing College.

12. At the age of eighty years, he is now pastor of the eighty year old Water Tower Baptist Church, the fifth largest Baptist Church in St. Louis, and serving as executive administrator and chaplain of the Fountain City Retirement Home in Bridgeton, Missouri. In his spare time he edits The Water Tower Witness for his church, and the Friendly Visitor for his retirement home—each of these are weekly publications. He is wondering if any one has an odd job they could give him!

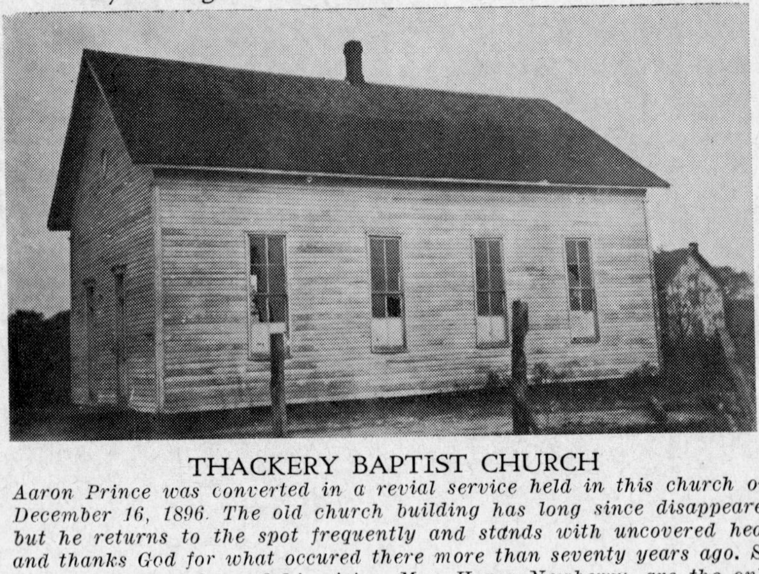

THACKERY BAPTIST CHURCH

Aaron Prince was converted in a revial service held in this church on December 16, 1896. The old church building has long since disappeared but he returns to the spot frequently and stands with uncovered head and thanks God for what occured there more than seventy years ago. So far as he knows he and his sister, Mrs. Harry Newberry, are the only persons now living on earth who were present at that service.

II.

THE EARLY YEARS

The story of the early years of Aaron Prince is filled with interesting things and we feel that this book would not be complete if these were omitted.

Childhood Days

Aaron Prince spent his childhood days in Wayne, Gallatin, Hamilton and White Counties in Illinois, and he was never beyond the limits of these counties until he was a grown man. His first day in public school was in Ridgeway, Illinois, in 1894. His father was pastor of the First Baptist Church, and the founder and first editor of the Ridgeway News—the paper he started in 1893, and which has been published weekly since that time.

The lad and his father were inseparable companions, and often talked together about God, the Bible and the way of salvation. The young lad spent much time in the printing office and learned much about the art of printing. Whether in the shop, or in the home, or going along the street, the boy was always asking questions about God and the things pertaining to the Kingdom of God and the Christian life. These father and son conferences were kept up at intervals until the father went home to be with the Lord.

The Prince family moved from place to place as the work of the preacher father required, and lived at times in town and at other times in the country. There were times during their school days when the children walked a distance of as much as three miles to school each morning and back at night. This was before school busses had been invented and before it ever occurred to people that a trip of five or six miles per day, in all kinds of weather, was too much for children to walk. Instead of eating at noon in a school cafeteria, the pupils carried their lunches to school in half-gallon tin pails. Some students had full dinner pails of delicious food. The Prince children's lunch pails sometimes contained only square pieces of corn bread with butter and molasses inside. At hog-killing time they fared better. The piece de resistance then was a chunk of home-made pork sausage deep in that piece of corn bread. Big homemade cucumber pickles and slices of onions added to the delights of the meal.

The childhood home of Aaron Prince had its family altar. Some of the most vivid memories of his life center around the family altar of that modest home. His mother was a minister's daughter, a minister's wife, and a minister's mother, and, above all, a woman of prayer. His father came of a long line of preachers, and was a faithful minister for forty-two years, in Southern Illinois. In the midst of poverty they prayed. When the chores were finished and night had come, the family gathered in the living room and the Bible was read and prayer was offered. The first public prayer that Aaron Prince ever offered was at that family altar, soon after his conversion. God pity the child who has never known the blessings of a family worship service! Robert Burns sketched a meaningful word picture of such a scene, and then wrote—

> From scenes like these, Old Scotia's grandeur springs,
> That makes her loved at home, revered abroad;
> Princes and Lords are but the breath of Kings,
> "An honest man's the noblest work of God."

This is the first picture of Dr. Prince. His father, mother, and sister are with him. He calls attention to the "index finger" of the right hand, and calls it his "preaching finger."

He was just an ordinary poor boy in childhood's years, always of serious mind and habits. He states that he has been a preacher from the time he was tall enough to stand behind his "pulpit," the seat of a straight-backed chair, and practice the prescribed manner of sermonizing in those days . . . . yelling at the top of his voice and pounding upon an open Bible. His ministry was quite successful so far as converts were concerned for every time it rained he had baptismal services in the old pond and the puddles of water. All the cats and dogs and chickens he could catch were solemnly carried out into the water and immersed. Since he was the oldest child in a family of eight, he was able to enforce conversion on his younger brothers and sisters as often as he ran out of other candidates for baptism. He had many preaching services.

If any of their pets died, he had funeral services. He says that the angels must have looked on with interest for he was always sure that they were near during those services. Often he went out into the woods all alone and solemnly preached to an imaginary crowd of hundreds and did the baptizings. He stood up in the manger in the barn and preached to the horses; in the chicken house he preached to the chickens; and he even converted the hog pens into sanctuaries. It is said that Henry Clay addressed the cabbage heads in his mother's garden, dreaming that these were United States Senators. If there had been a cabbage patch on the place, no doubt this aspiring young preacher would have addressed himself to the rows of cabbage heads. He might have worried more over the indifference found here than over the active objections in the barnyard. Two or three old roosters objected to his brand of theology, especially its ordinances, and he had to consign them to the nether regions, but the revivals went on just the same. He had to run down his candidates and carry them into the water. They got out of their own accord when he turned them loose and did not remain for the collection or benediction. They were verbose in their testimony as they got out of the baptistry.

The first time he saw the observance of the Lord's Supper the deacons passed by the hungry boy and did not offer him any bread. A bit later they came along with the one and only glass, in which the elders had washed their whiskers, but they didn't offer it to him either. When he and his father reached home after the service, he ran in and asked his mother whether dinner was ready. He told her that they had served a little bite at the church but that he did not get any of it.*

He vividly recalls the first time death came to his home. He was twelve years of age at that time. The sun dawned in a cloudless sky on that fateful day. All had been well in the little home that Saturday morning when his father left for his preaching appointment twenty miles away. But at noon that day a little brother became seriously ill, and before the sun set in the west that evening, little brother had gone to be with the Lord. This was the hardest blow the family had known. Kind-hearted neighbors came and stayed with them, ministering to them in their sorrow. The father was summoned and hastened home. The night which followed that day was a night unlike any other they had ever known. This experience made a lasting impression on the twelve-year-old elder brother.

It had always been his custom, wherever the family lived, to

---

* There was a pasture lot just over the back-yard fence of the boyhood home of Aaron Prince. His mother had told him to stay out of that lot. He climbed over the fence one day and started across the lot. Presently he saw the old billy-goat coming in his direction with majestic steps and with each step a significant shake of his head. The frightened boy started for the fence and the goat also started in the same direction at the same time. They met at the fence. The goat helped him over the fence. As fate would have it, his mother came along just as the goat kissed him good-bye. The mother examined the boy, surveyed the situation and then proceeded to practice the art of laying on of hands. The boy states that his mother believed in applied psychology and that she was exceedingly graceful and skillful in the matter of the laying on of hands. He also states that he did not baptize the goat!

have his secret place for prayer. At this time his special spot was under an old apple tree at the back of the orchard. When the weather permitted, he would repair to this altar of prayer under cover of darkness and give himself to thought and prayer. On this eventful night he went to his sacred altar and looked up through the branches of the tree to the stars of heaven seeking to learn why little brother had gone away. God was very near the boy who knelt under the tree that night.*

The old apple tree — his place of prayer

Out of a home of prayer, came a boy who has felt throughout the years the touch of the Master's hand on his heart and life and has ever sought the will of God in every matter. In this way the lives of Godly parents reach far into the future to shine upon the paths of men, and the waves of influence

* Dr. Prince has returned to his old home place as opportunity has afforded in later years. One by one the familiar landmarks have disappeared, and at last only one remained. The one remaining landmark was the old apple tree where he used to pray. It is significant that his altar of prayer should be the last remaining landmark to disappear, signifying that only that which is eternal is important. The old apple tree stood in the midst of a cornfield when this picture was taken. A cedar tree which stood seventy years ago in front of the home of his grandfather near Thackery, Illinois, still stands—the only remaining landmark of that old home.

from such homes roll on to wash the shore of eternity. Thank God for Christian homes.

Calvin Coolidge said not long before his death: "The true civic center of our municipalities will be found not in some towering edifice with stately approaches, nor in broad avenues flanked with magnificent mansions, but around the family altar of the American home, the source of that strength which has marked our national character, where above all else is cherished a faith in the things not seen."

Conversion and Baptism

One of the most joyful experiences of life is realized in relating one's Christian experience, and yet it is a most difficult task. It is not possible to relate it all in words. One can state the case up to a certain point and then jump over and continue the story on the other side, but there is a little part of the experience between these two that one cannot adequately relate. This is the part which God does as we seek salvation. Because it is a work of God, man cannot adequately interpret it. Apart from this experience with God, there is no salvation; neither is there any testimony worthy of being related. Let him tell you how Jesus came into his heart. Here it is in an editorial from the Baptist Visitor, a weekly paper which he published for years:

> One evening while my father was away on a preaching tour, my mother called me to her knee and read to me the last two chapters of the Bible. She told me of that wonderful City of God. It was all very interesting and wonderful to me. After she had read the chapters and talked with me, we knelt in prayer and my mother talked to God in such a simple manner that, while I could not understand it, yet I knew that God was somewhere near. This is the first memory of a consciousness of God which comes out of my childhood years and I shall never lose it in the boundless depths of eternity.

For some two or three years I pondered these things in my heart and asked my father and mother many questions. We moved to a country home near Thackery, Illinois in the meanwhile, and a revival meeting was started at New Hope Baptist Church, some two miles away. My father was the pastor and was doing the preaching in this meeting. I went to the services with him in the evenings and listened with greatest interest. The appeals of the sermons, and songs, and the prayers shook my soul to its very depths and I was conscious of the drawing power of the cross of Christ and of the Spirit of God. I wanted to be saved. No one said anything to me. It is probable the Christian people never thought of a child having an interest in this matter. New converts of those days in that community were grown people. The meeting closed, leaving upon me an undying impression of that closing service. This was the autumn of 1896. I was nine years of age at that time.

A strange experience came to me about the time this meeting closed. I had a very dear friend, a little crippled lad. He was my playmate. One day the word came that he was ill and in a brief time the word came from the sick room that he was dead. I was stunned by this tragedy. It was the first time death had ever come very near to me. I went over to the home of my friend and stood and looked at his pale, cold face. I came out of that room a sadder and wiser boy. For the first time the fact that I must some day go into the valley of death came to me and I was overwhelmed by the thought.

In those dark days of grief my heart was torn between the loss of my friend and the staggering fact of death lurking somewhere in the shadows for me. I put sundry and various questions to my parents as we sat by the fireside in the evenings, and I roamed the fields and woods in the daytime trying to adjust myself to the new things which had come into my life.

At this time I came face to face with another fact. I knew from what I had read in the Bible and from conversations with my parents that the spirit of my little friend lived on somewhere. I tried to draw aside the curtain as I walked and meditated. This brought another discovery utterly incomprehensible to me. I discovered that there was something within man which is beyond the power of death and must live on forever. This made me long inexpressibly for salvation.

About this time a revival meeting began at Thackery Baptist Church. My father was assisting the pastor, Elder J. W.

Allen, in this meeting. I went to the services. I sat quietly in the pew and watched with quickened senses all that went on about me. As those faithful saints of God talked to Him in prayer, I trembled, and in my childish heart I knew that God was somewhere near. I longed for peace. I wanted someone to talk to me, but I was left unnoticed. I spent hours in the fields and woods for days trying to find God in prayer. There was great comfort in these efforts to pray but not the peace I sought.

I was permitted to leave the public school one morning to attend the day service. This was the sixteenth day of December, 1896. My father preached that morning; and when the invitation was given, a number went forward to the altar of prayer. I wanted to go. Presently my mother came down the aisle and put her arms about her boy and asked him to come to Jesus. No sweeter invitation had ever come to me. I knelt at that altar while the congregation sang and prayed. My mother, my grandmother, and my father knelt about me. My mother's arms were about me. I was trying to pray. I was really trying everything I knew to save myself.

My mother's words brought the light to me. In the midst of my agony of soul, she said: "My son, you cannot save yourself. You must surrender completely to Jesus." I looked up to Jesus just then and said, "Here, Lord, I give myself to Thee, it's all that I can do." With that complete surrender, and through faith, there came that sweet peace I had so long sought. Heaven seemed to be all about the mercy seat. The glory of God was there as on the mercy seat of old. The congregation was singing, "At the Cross, At the Cross, Where I first saw the Light, and the burden of my heart rolled away." This had been sung many times in the meeting but I knew a new meaning as I heard it at that hour.

Aaron Prince presented himself for membership in New Hope Baptist Church, two miles southwest of Thackery, Illinois, on Saturday before the fourth Sunday in January, 1897. His father, pastor of the church, preached and gave the invitation at that service. Rev. John B. Smith, a prominent Baptist preacher of Southern Illinois, was present and was invited to examine the young convert as to his profession of faith and fitness for church membership. After being questioned, the boy was approved for baptism.

New Hope Church

As was the custom, the baptismal service was deferred until the arrival of warm weather. By May, the chill of winter had gone from the ponds and streams, and Pastor Peter Prince administered the ordinance of baptism at the regular fourth Sunday service. But times had been hard in the Prince household that year, and so the preacher's son could not be baptized because he did not have a change of clothes to put on to wear home after the ceremony. He went out into the wood lot and sat on a log and cried while the baptismal service was in progress at the other end of the lot. His mother came out and sat on that log and cried with him. But where there's a will, there is a way. By careful planning and management, the mother and father provided the necessary extra clothing by the time a second baptismal service was held on the third Sunday in June, 1897, in a pond on the J. B. Hawthorne farm three miles east of McLeansboro, Illinois. And so, on that day, a very happy boy was baptized by his earthly father in obedience to the command of his Heavenly Father.

ALTAR OF DEDICATION

There should be at least two mountain peaks in every life—one the Mount of Regeneration and the other the Mount of Dedication of self and life to God. Aaron Prince had come to the first at the age of nine years when he found Christ as his Saviour at an old-fashioned mourner's bench, in an old-fashioned revival, where old-fashioned sinners were coming to Jesus in the old-fashioned way. He reached the second peak three years later. By this time the family had moved to White County, Illinois, and lived on a farm two miles south of Burnt Prairie. He says, "Every boy ought to have the privilege of growing up on a farm. The experience can contribute much to one's life."

It was always his custom to pray much when he was alone. He was the oldest child, and because of the illness of his father he had the responsibility of planting, cultivating, and harvesting the crops. As he followed the plow or reaped the wheat or harvested the corn, he was always praying.

It happened that his mother sent him to town one afternoon in early spring to sell two dozen eggs at five cents a dozen and purchase one pound of coffee with the proceeds. He was returning from town in the late afternoon, praying as he walked homeward. It was at this hour that he came to his Mount of Dedication. The gentle spring days had thawed out the frozen earth and melted the bit of snow that lingered in the cracks and crevices. The little streams were bank-full of surging waters. He came to such a stream a half mile from home. He stood beside the stream watching the swirling waters go by. He knew his geography well enough to know that this stream emptied into another, and that stream into the Little Wabash River, and on into the Ohio, down the Mississippi, into the Gulf, and eventually to the seven seas of the world. The twelve-year-old philosopher stood beside the stream and compared the course of that water to the course of his own life, reflecting on how his life could run on and outward until its influence would wash the shores of eternity.

He took off his cap, lifted his tear-filled eyes toward heaven, and said: "Lord, here I am, a mere lad with years stretching forth before me—with a life that I can throw away in idleness, and stain with sin, or dedicate to that which is highest and holiest and best. Lord, here and now I offer to Thee this life of mine—in holy dedication to Thee and Thy cause, and in a steadfast and sustained consecration to Thee until life's last earthly hour." Borden of Yale said much the same thing in these words:

> Lord Jesus, I take my hands off, as far as my life is concerned. I put Thee on the throne of my heart. Change, cleanse, use me as Thou shalt choose. I take the full power of Thy Spirit. I thank Thee. May never know a tithe of the result until Morning.

The years have come and gone, sixty-eight of them, but Dr. Prince has never gone back on that dedication by the side of the brook. Today, even as on that faraway day, his life and his all are on the altar for God. His daily prayer is that God will continue to use him until life is over.

> "Happy if with my latest breath,
> I may but speak His name,
> Preach Christ in life, and gasp in death,
> Behold! Behold the lamb!"

CALL TO PREACH

Beyond any question of doubt, one of the greatest experiences of the life of any one is the call to preach the "unsearchable riches of Christ." One might be able to shake the confidence of Dr. Prince in the reality of other experiences of his life but never in his divine call to the work of the ministry. It has ever been his conviction that no man has any right to any pulpit unless he is fortified by a conviction as deep as life itself that he is called of God to preach the Gospel. God has reserved to Himself the task of calling His ministers and of placing them in their pulpits. Let every man who assays to stand behind the sacred desk make sure of his divine credentials.

It is probably true that many of our problems in our churches begin at this point. We have men who have been called by other men. Dr. Prince says that he has never at any time said to any man, "God is calling you to preach." It has been his conviction that if God wants a man in the ministry He has a way of getting him into that work.

There is another thing, he says, that has been worn thread-bare and ragged, and that is the statement of those who say that they "fought the call" to preach or that they "surrendered" to the call to the ministry. If there is any ground for such statements, it is the fault of men, and not of God.

Let all men know that here is one man who never engaged God in battle over the matter of a call to preach. He has held from life's early days that all he has and is belongs to God, and that God has a sovereign right to demand his best and his all. When Isaiah, beholding the display of the glory of God in the Temple, heard the voice of God saying, "Whom shall I send, and who will go for us?" he replied, "Here am I, send me." Here is a good scripture for study by men who claim to have fought God's call. A good vision of God takes all the fight out of any man.

Thank God for the clear and wide-open spaces on the farm. Many of the deep and abiding experiences of Dr. Prince came when he was alone in the fields. This was true when God called him to preach. He had been sent on an errand to the home of a neighbor, one-half mile south of his home. It was a bitter winter day. The snow was falling and the wind was from the north. There was no road. He was crossing the field. On his return, facing the north wind was a very uncomfortable experience. He stopped and stood behind a tree while rubbing his ears and cheeks, which seemed in danger of freezing. As he stood on the south side of the tree—all this is very vivid to him—with his back to the tree and his face to the south, he was praying as was always his custom when alone in the field. He was praying about how to invest his life. This was the tenth day of January, 1901, and exactly ten days after his fourteenth birthday.

God passed by that day. There was no open vision, no voice, no sound of footsteps, but there was a deep, earth-shattering conviction, as deep as life itself, and as strong as if there had been a vision and a voice calling him into the work of the ministry. Tears were streaming down his cheeks and tears have ever been near the surface when he has stood in the presence of God. With Jacob, he was saying: "Surely the Lord is in this place; and I knew it not . . . How dreadful is this place! This is none other than the house of God, and this is the gate of heaven." As clearly as if an audible voice was speaking, he heard the Lord saying, "To this end you were born, and for this purpose you have come into the world, to preach my Gospel to dying men." Was there any fighting a call on his part? There was none. He gladly said: "Lord, here am I, send me."

Paul was a matchless preacher, second only to our Lord. He did not "fight" the call to preach. He was fortified by the fact that he was born to preach. He says: "But when it pleased God, who separated me from my mother's womb, and called me by His grace, to reveal His Son in me, that I might preach

Him among the heathen, immediately I conferred not with flesh and blood . . ." (Gal. 1:15-16). Dr. Prince feels that his name is not worthy to be mentioned in the same breath with the name of Paul, but he requests that he, who is "less than the least of all saints," be allowed to say that his response to God's call is the same as that of Paul, and with great humility he can say that the conviction of his soul is that he, too, was *born to preach.* He was and is still "obedient to the heavenly vision."

In the above passage from Galatians, Paul goes on to say that after he was called to preach, he conferred not with flesh and blood, nor went up to Jerusalem to discuss the matter with those who were already apostles, but that he went into Arabia. There all alone he spent probably three years, recasting all his theological thinking. The young Prince boy, after his call to preach, spent more time in the fields alone with God. For some time he took no one into his confidence, seeking not the counsel of men but only the companionship of God. After a while, he told his mother, but for three years he told no one else of his call. During this period he went forward in companionship with God, read his Bible much and spent time in prayer. He felt assured that the God who had called him and predestinated him to this work would open the way for him. He found perfect peace in this conviction, and subsequent events proved the merits of his decision and brought the reward for his patient waiting.

Let us close this chapter with the words of G. Campbell Morgan, who when commenting on the choosing of the Twelve (Luke 6:12-19), said: "When He called them, He chose from them, twelve. That was election. That was selection. This was the act of absolute sovereignty. He did not call all His disciples and take them into consultation. He made his own selection, and it was the selection of eternal wisdom. He chose the right men . . . . I never read this story without gathering a great deal of comfort from it. When He chose these men, the responsibility of choice rested on Him, and not on them. Now, supposing I had been one of the twelve. From that day forward, and growingly, as the years passed, I should have wondered why He chose me. I wonder at the fact as it is. But He did choose me, and that is enough for me; the responsibility is on Him. Oh, the comfort of it. Oh, the strength of it. If a man holds any office in the Christian Church, whether preacher, elder, or deacon, and God did not choose him, God pity Him. If He did, and the man knows it in his deepest soul, that is the secret of courage, that is the secret of strength. He chose me. I am not speaking for effect. I am saying the deepest thing in my soul."

Paul never wavered in his conviction that God separated him from his mother's womb, and called him by His grace . . . that he might preach. G. Campbell Morgan was comforted by the thought that God did choose him, and that the responsibility for this choice was upon God, though Morgan marvelled at it all. The secret of the strength of Aaron Prince lies in the deep and ever-abiding conviction that he was *born to preach,* called of God to preach, and hence he can say: "By the grace of God, I am what I am: and His grace which was bestowed upon me, was not in vain."

III.

BEGINNINGS OF HIS WORK

Two great sorrows came into the life of young A. E. Prince in the year 1903. His grandfather Young, long time preacher, was killed by a fall from a horse on Decoration Day. A second sorrow followed shortly, for Death came again and took away another little brother on October 22, 1903.

The home on Pig Ridge where he lived when he traveled to Barnhill to preach his first sermon.

In the settlement of his grandfather's estate, his mother had fallen heir to a parcel of land and the house in which the grandfather lived on Pig Ridge. The Prince family moved into this house on June 3, 1903.

Pig Ridge was the name given to a little ridge of land on the border of the lowlands of the Skillet Fork River seven miles southwest of Fairfield. From whence the name came is not known. Their home was in the midst of Pig Ridge. The inhabitants of that land were like Goldsmith's village preacher in one respect at least, namely, they "had not changed nor wished to change their place." Whatever was good for their grandfathers was good enough for them.

The lowland soil was fairly rich, but much of it was under water every time the Skillet Fork River overflowed. From the front porch of their home they could see the backwater one-eighth of a mile away. Pig Ridge was headquarters for mosquitoes. Chinch bugs ate the corn that cut worms did not take. Potato bugs ate the potatoes, and cabbage worms ate the cabbage. The scenery was in no sense attractive in those days. The casual observer, passing through the one road that led in and out from the neighborhood could well have asked: "Can any good thing come out of Pig Ridge?"

The Boy From Pig Ridge

A boy came out of Pig Ridge! On January 8, 1904, a seventeen-year-old boy with Bible in hand walked four miles to Hubbard Switch on the Baltimore and Ohio Railroad and rode three miles on the late afternoon train to Barnhill, Illinois, a small village six miles south of Fairfield. A dream of some three years was about to come true. In Barnhill there was in progress a revival meeting conducted by the pastor, Rev. Sylvester Howell. Two days earlier, on January 6, the boy from Pig Ridge and his friend, Mr. Roy Gantz, had gone to the revival service. They returned for the service the following evening and, arriving early, found only two people there ahead of them. When the boy sat down beside the stove to warm,

The "boy preacher" at 17 years of age.

Pastor Howell came and sat in the seat beside him and Deacon George Singletary on the seat in front of him and said: "We want to ask you a question—Did you ever feel that God has called you to preach?" Without a moment's hesitation he replied that he was definitely called to preach. The pastor said, "Praise the Lord," and the deacon said, "We were sure of this when we saw you for the first time last night." The pastor said, "We want you to preach your first sermon tomorrow night in this revival." So on January 8, 1904, at about 3 p.m., a boy from Pig Ridge walked four miles and traveled three miles by train to Barnhill. When the time came for the service to begin that Friday night, the church was crowded to capacity and people were standing in the cold outside the doors and windows. The Boy from Pig Ridge stood up and read his text, "Prepare to meet thy God" (Amos 4:12), and poured out his soul to the people, many of whom were weeping. It was a great service. And so it was that the boy who had preached to the horses, the chickens and the pigs stood with fear and trembling and preached to a great congregation of people. The revival continued and the young man preached over Sunday. A blizzard closed the revival Monday night.

Dr. Prince says he has never ceased to wonder why he was chosen to be a minister. Just why God should lay his hand on a mere boy, out on a farm, from a home of poverty, and with such limited opportunities has never been very clear to him, unless it might be said to be a demonstration of what God can do with a life that is yielded to Him.

He has several "outlines" of his early sermons—in the original handwriting on pages of a little note book. Two scraps of paper he values highly. One was written on December 16, 1900, and indicated the heart and thought of a boy on whom God had laid His hand. The boy wrote . . . .

> "Four years ago today I professed a hope in Christ Jesus. I this year enter my teens. God only knows whether I will live till I am past them."

The other highly valued scrap of paper is the "outline" of his first sermon, (if it might be dignified by being called an "outline"). He has released it—not as a model of sermonic literature, but, as he said, to show that "if God can use a boy who could not do any better than that, surely He can use many others today." This little "outline" was written in pencil on both sides of a sheet of small notebook paper. Here is the "outline" which was the "running gears" of what he calls a tear-jerking sermon:

Text Amos 4:12
A Solemn Warning
An Exhortation to Repentance
Two divisions of people—saved and unsaved.
  Christ died for men.

Through the merits of His blood we can prepare.
Men need preparation—because all are sinners.
The wages of sin is death.
Some have promised to meet mother.
PREPARE TO MEET THY GOD.

Barnhill Baptist Church, in conference assembled at the old-fashioned Saturday afternoon business session on January 9, 1904, licensed the young boy to preach the Gospel and exercise his gifts in the work of the ministry.

ORDINATION

The people of Barnhill Church lost no time in setting apart the "Boy Preacher" to the full work of the Gospel Ministry. At the February business session it was voted to call a council to ordain him to the work of the ministry at the March meeting of the church. A big flood came the night before the council was to meet and no one could get to Barnhill. At the April business session another call was made for a council to convene on Saturday before the fifth Sunday in May. This council, convening at 7 p.m. on Saturday, May 28, conducted a three-hour examination of the candidate and met again at 9 a.m. on Sunday, May 29, 1904, for two more hours of examination, after which the young man was ordained. The council was composed of the following ministers and deacons:

Antioch—Deacon Charles Walters
Barnhill Church—Rev. Peter Prince
Deacons—George W. Singletary
Noah Renfrow
Charles Singletary
William Atteberry
J. D. Tucker
Mt. Zion—Rev. Sylvester Howell
Deacons—Sam Pilcher
Lewis Groves
Pleasant Hill—Deacon W. L. Bishop
Pleasant Grove—Deacon Joseph Bonner
Sims—Rev. W. J. Anderson
Deacons—A. M. Singletary
J. S. Bright

The Council was organized by the election of Rev. W. J. Anderson, Moderator, and Deacon J. S. Bright, Clerk. The following program was adopted and carried out:

Presentation of the candidate by the deacons of Barnhill Baptist Church
Examination led by Rev. W. J. Anderson
Ordination prayer—Rev. Sylvester Howell, Pastor Barnhill Church
Imposition of hands by council
Charge to Candidate—Deacon George W. Singletary
Charge to Church—Rev. Peter Prince
Presentation of Bible—Deacon J. S. Bright
Ordination Sermon—Rev. W. J. Anderson

The Candidate was asked to give statement of his Christian experience and call to the ministry before the ordination prayer and the imposition of hands which followed.

As he knelt in the altar of Barnhill Baptist Church on that eventful Sunday morning, with the members of the council all about him, he registered a vow in heaven that he would at all times faithfully proclaim the whole counsel of God and ever regard the Bible as the divinely inspired Word of God, and that if the time ever came when he did not so regard the Word of God and so preach Christ, he would vacate the pulpit. To this vow he has ever remained faithful.

Every man on the council of ordination on that far away day is now in the Father's house on high. Dr. Prince returned to Barnhill on Sunday, May 30, 1954, to fulfill a dream of fifty years, which was to return to the old church and preach his fiftieth anniversary sermon there. He preached to a crowded house on the subject, "The Message We Preach." There were only three people at this service who heard his first sermon fifty years ago. Since that time these also have crossed over to the Father's house on high. The old church building burned not long after this anniversary service, and a new building now stands on the spot where the old church stood.

PREACHING IN THE HORSE-AND-BUGGY DAYS

Aaron Prince did not select the name "Boy Preacher." That name was given him by the newspapers—both the religious press and the secular press. A preacher barely seventeen years old had never been seen in all that part of the world, and wherever he preached there were those who came purely out of curiosity. In those days people went to church on horse back, in wagons and buggies, and on foot. My, how he would love to live those days over again!

He had neither horse, buggy, nor wagon. He walked to many of his engagements, trudging along the road with Bible in hand. He had little or no money for clothes. On the day of his ordination he wore a pair of shoes about two sizes too large, a coat of one color and trousers of another, and an old man's straw hat. This was his garb until winter stowed the straw hat away. Verily those were the "horse and buggy days," and the "Boy Wonder," as some people called him, moved about somewhat fearfully and wonderfully arrayed.

He preached in church buildings, in homes, in stores, in the open air—in fact, anywhere he was invited. And sometimes, without invitation, he preached on street corners. He knew a Saviour and he wanted to tell about Him.

His first regular appointment came when Mr. John Tice asked him to preach regularly once-a-month on Saturday nights, Sunday morning, and Sunday night, under the shade trees on the Tice farm. This farm was two and one-half miles northeast of Merriam, in Wayne County, Illinois. The men of the neighborhood cut logs into blocks about eighteen inches long, set them on end, and laid planks across them for seats. The preacher preached to good congregations there throughout the summer of 1904.

His First Pastorate

By the end of the summer he had more calls than he could accept. His first church was Pleasant Hill, in Mt. Erie Association, near the town of Mt. Erie, Illinois. He visited this church in September and preached to a congregation of seven people. A call was extended at the close of the service for once-a-month services at $4.00 per month. Samaria Church and Unity Church, both near Albion, and Brown's Church, all three in Edwards County, called him about this same time; and he was off to full-time work. Other calls came but could not be accepted.

His First Revival

His first revival was held in October, 1904 in Samaria Church, five miles northwest of Albion. The meeting continued two weeks. Four people were saved and all united with the church for baptism, and he did his first baptizing in the Little Wabash River on the closing day of the meeting.

His First Funeral

He conducted his first funeral service on Sunday, November 13, 1904 at the home of J. S. Graham near Mt. Erie, Illinois. The deceased was Ignatious Walker, seventy-five years of age and widely known in and around Mt. Erie. The burial was in Walker Cemetery.

His First Wedding

He was barely eighteen years of age when he officiated at his first marriage service. This was a large wedding at the Collins' home, not far from Samaria church, when Miss Armada Collins and Mr. Herbert Conley were united in marriage. During the ceremony the youthful preacher was a bit disturbed by what he thought was an occasional snicker in the crowd, fearful that he was not performing in the accepted manner for such occasions. He learned later that it was sobs instead of snickers. This discovery gave a speck of comfort to the young divine and he was encouraged to believe that he might some day exceed his most sanguine expectations as a marrying parson.

His First Great Revival

The greatest revival in the experience of the "Boy Preacher" occurred at Pleasant Grove Baptist Church, five miles southeast of Fairfield, in January-February, 1906. Rev. W. H. McCann, of Albion, was pastor at Pleasant Grove. A revival broke out. Pastor McCann requested the church to secure the "Boy Preacher" to assist in the meeting. A great revival followed and the whole community was stirred as never before nor since in the history of the church. The revival continued 24 days. Services began at 10:00 a.m. and 7:00 p.m. and each service lasted four hours. The church was crowded to capacity in spite of bitter winter weather. Many were saved, and many others rededicated their lives. There was shouting at almost every service. One mother, told that her boy had just been saved, shouted all over the house, but finally found that there was a mistake and that it was another boy, not her boy who had been saved. Her boy was saved later. Scores of people who were saved in that meeting now sleep in the church yard at old Pleasant Grove.

His Career as Teacher

From 1904 to 1910 the rapidly developing young preacher served quarter-time and half-time churches. During this time he taught school for two years (1906-1908) at Fairview school in Wayne County. He had a unique experience there. A revival was started in Lebanon Presbyterian Church near Fairview.

There was not a Christian in his school when the revival began. The young preacher was asked to dismiss school and help in the revival. Every pupil of accountable age was saved during that three weeks' revival. Education was the hand-maiden of religion in those days.

His Great Teachers

Two men did more to influence his life and prepare him for the ministry than all others whose paths crossed his path in those early years. One was his father, Rev. Peter Prince. The "Boy Preacher" began early in life to ask his father questions about the Bible and religion. After the son entered the ministry they had many conversations about the work of the ministry. The faith of the young preacher was confirmed by these hours of fellowship and conferences, and he was taught many things about Bible doctrine, the art of preaching and church administration.

The other man who taught the young preacher much during this period was Rev. W. H. McCann, the father of Dr. O. M. McCann of East St. Louis. The seventeen-year-old preacher was called to the pastorate of Unity Baptist Church, southwest of Albion, and the McCann family held membership in this church. The "Boy Preacher" made his monthly trips to fill his preaching engagements at Unity, and was always a guest on Saturday and Sunday nights in the McCann home. The distinguished physician, now of East St. Louis, Illinois, and who is now the family physician of Dr. Prince, was a thirteen year old lad at that time in that Edwards County farm home. Many mornings the young preacher was awakened by his host about 4:00 o'clock for another session of theological training. While the young preacher would lie in bed, his host would walk the floor and deliver a two-hour lecture in homiletics, ministerial ethics, and Biblical instruction. There is no way to measure fully the impact of the life of that aged preacher upon the young man who was a guest month by month in his home. Paul was brought up at the feet of Gamaliel, but the "Boy Preacher" was brought up at the feet of two of the best and greatest theologians in Southern Illinois. Their courses of instruction to him substituted well for seminary courses. Throughout his ministry Dr. Prince has followed the road chartered for him by these noble men of God, and states that no course in theology, pursued by him in later years, was nearly so profitable as the teaching of these distinguished ministers. He refers to this as his chimney-corner seminary.

TAKING A WIFE

Aaron Prince never left the home of his childhood—the home left him! The family lived on a thirty-six acre farm two miles south of Fairfield. His father was called to the pastorate of the First Baptist Church, Glasford, Illinois, and the family moved to that city. The young preacher was twenty-two years of age at that time, and those were his last days in his boyhood home. He was pastor of some churches in Southern Illinois and stayed with his work.

Mention has already been made of the great revival in Pleasant Grove Baptist Church, southeast of Fairfield. When the church became pastorless in the fall of 1907 he was called to serve as pastor for half-time work. There was in that church a noble family that was destined to have a great impact on his life. Deacon Joseph Bonner was one of the best of men and had a lovely family of two sons and four daughters who grew to adulthood. Four of these—John, Perry, Pearl and Iva were saved in the big revival in January, 1907. Pearl came to the old-fashioned altar in the meeting in both morning and evening services for about two weeks and was always the first to respond to the invitation each time. She was converted in a season of prayer in her own home on Sunday before the revival closed. A number of people had gone to the Bonner home for dinner that Sunday and a long prayer service was in progress in the parlor downstairs when she was saved all alone upstairs.

During his second year as pastor, the young preacher and Pearl found much of common interest in each other. No one among the church people was aware of this fact. The preacher was a guest in the Bonner home on Sunday night once a month, and at the home of Mr. and Mrs. Frank Simpson on the alternate Sunday nights. Mrs. Simpson was Pearl's sister. The preacher and Pearl did their "courting" on these Sunday nights. So carefully was the secret guarded that it was not known among the church people until the invitations to the wedding were mailed in August, 1909.

On Tuesday, August 24, 1909, at 8 p.m., in the home of the bride's widowed mother, occurred the marriage of Miss Pearl Bonner and the "Boy Preacher." The ceremony was performed by Rev. W. H. McCann in the parlor of the Bonner home seven miles southeast of Fairfield, Illinois. The young couple began housekeeping in a three-room house in Norris City, Illinois, where the groom was serving half-time as pastor of the First Baptist Church of Norris City, and also, quarter-time at Saline Creek near Shawneetown and Blue Mound Church near Carmi. This was the beginning of a happy marriage union of about two score years.

Pearl Bonner Prince was one of the noblest and best of women. She was a true companion, a devout Christian, and a faithful servant of our Lord. She was one of the most patient and devoted of mothers. Those who knew her best and loved her most cannot recall an unkind word ever spoken by her.

Pearl Bonner Prince at the time of her marriage to the "boy preacher."

Whatever hardship or trial that came to them in the work of her husband was borne by her and shared by her in the noblest manner.

Her thought was ever for her Lord, her husband and his work, and her house and the children. She was inflexible in her own righteous conduct, but charitable toward the short-comings of others; modest to timidity in her estimation of her own worth and attainments, but high in her estimation and appreciation of the abilities and attainments of others. It was her happy privilege to be the mother of six children and to see them grow to maturity. All of them have filled and are filling well their places in their chosen fields of service, and have walked in the ways of their mother in the fear of God.

This faithful mother passed away October 18, 1946, and was laid to rest in Grand View Cemetery in Hannibal, Missouri.

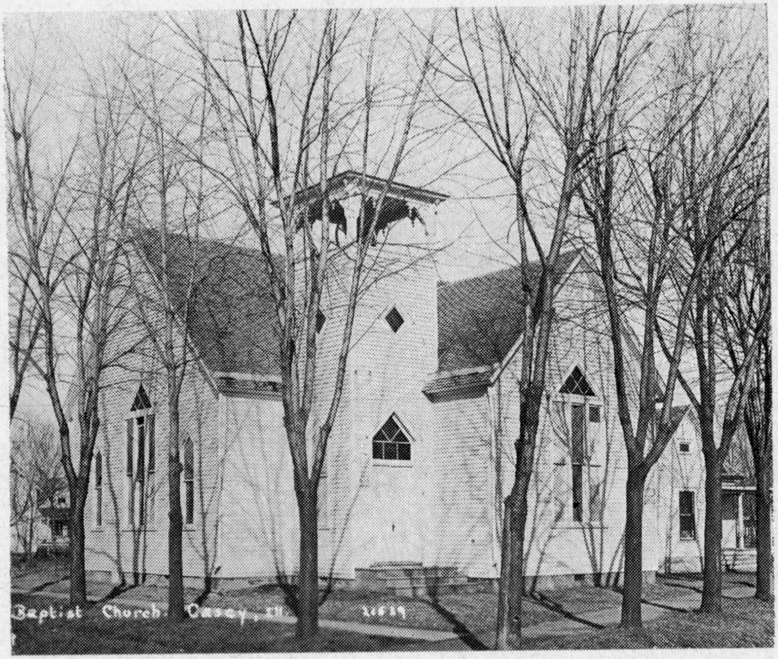

The First Baptist Church, Casey, Illinois, was the first full time pastorate of Aaron Prince. This building was recently demolished and a beautiful and commodious building now stands on this spot.

IV.

THE WIDENING HORIZONS

Just at this point, we come to a change in the work of the young preacher. Heretofore he had served rural and village churches—a work he enjoyed very much. He grew to manhood in the country and was very much at home with rural people.

FIRST FULL TIME PASTORATE

The First Baptist Church, Casey, Illinois, called the young preacher February 2, 1910, and he and his young wife moved to that city on March 2, 1910. The call for half-time was soon extended to three-fourth's time and by autumn of that year he became full-time pastor at Casey—his first full-time pastorate. His work at Casey was fruitful. The work prospered and the people were happy. He says that the people patiently endured his short-comings through the week and his long standings on Sundays.

He held a revival in November which was outstanding in the history of the church. On the closing Sunday of the meeting, at 2:30 p.m., and owing to the fact that the church had no baptistry, he baptized eighteen candidates in a lake at the east edge of Casey. He remembers distinctly that on that cold November day the water was freezing at the edge of the lake.

His sermon barrel was soon empty and he was convinced that if he wanted to continue in the ministry and do effective work he would have to go to college. He began to pray for an opportunity to go to school. After eighteen months of service at Casey, he resigned to enter college.

Esther, his oldest child, was born in Casey on December 13, 1910.

ENTERING COLLEGE

In the fall of 1911 another dream came true; the preacher started to college. The little family moved to Ewing, Illinois, and into a four-room house, first door east of the First Baptist Church. Having been asked by the First Baptist Church of Casey to continue as pastor there, he commuted back and forth from Ewing to Casey during his first year in Ewing College. One interesting thing the preacher loves to relate is that when he moved into the house in Ewing and set up for housekeeping, put one little load of coal in the coal house, bought a small supply of groceries, and brought his wife and child to Ewing the next day, he had less than five dollars in his pocket. This was the beginning of a long, hard climb to education. The Casey church had gone back to half-time preaching and the First Baptist Church of Steeleville, Illinois, called him for the other two Sundays of each month. For one year, he served these churches on alternate Sundays.

Ewing College was a small school founded in 1867, and it had seen better days than were in evidence in 1911-1912. He enrolled on September 5, 1911, for a full course and was never happier than when he found himself realizing his dream for higher education. That year Dr. William A. Matthews of Chicago had succeeded Dr. J. A. Leavitt as president, and the school opened with a reduced student body. A group of ministerial students had walked out of the college in January, 1911, in a disagreement over some matters of doctrine and administration which was all but disastrous to the college at that time, and which proved to be the beginning of the end for the college.

Dr. Matthews left June 1, 1912, after one year of service as president. Most of the faculty he had brought to Ewing left, and a number of students went out with him. The College Board elected the twenty-five year old preacher as registrar of the college and asked him to take over the college—print the annual catalog, secure a faculty, and find as many students as he could. In fact, the desperate Board, feeling that he was the most capable person available, would have elected him president in spite of his youth and inexperience, but his modesty and good sense prohibited this being done.

First Church, Ewing

Moreover, the First Baptist Church of Ewing became pastorless during the summer of 1912 and called him for full time—his second full time pastorate. When the college opened the first week of September, 1912, he was pastor of this church, registrar of the college, teacher in the college offering as many subjects as any member of the faculty, and, student, carrying as many subjects as any student enrolled that year. He had assembled a good faculty, and one hundred fifty students were enrolled for the fall term. He was supremely happy in his work, associating with the faculty and students all week and preaching to all of them on Sunday.

One of the greatest revivals ever held in Ewing occurred in the early spring of 1913. The meeting ran one month and tremendously affected the city of Ewing and the faculty and students. All saw demonstrations of the power of God there. Four or five preachers did the preaching. There were four or five baptismal services during the revival. Faculty members and students and citizens of Ewing joined the church. The superintendent of Ewing Public Schools was won to Christ and baptized. The city marshall was won. It was a wonderful meeting. At the close of the revival every faculty member was a member of the local church, and almost every student. There were 44 professions of faith, 37 additions and 32 baptized.

A Dark Day in Ewing

A dark day came in October, 1914, in Ewing. The Board of Trustees held an all-day meeting and called all the faculty to meet with the Board in the First Baptist Church at 7:00 p.m. for "a very important announcement"—namely, that the Board had exhausted all its resources and had no money to pay salaries. Neither could the Board borrow any money. The faculty members were advised to accept positions elsewhere if openings could be found. Those who could find work left Ewing in a few days. A skeleton faculty stayed for the rest of the year and the college was kept open.

Another sad day in the life of the young preacher was the day he left Ewing. With no other course open to him, the erstwhile registrar, teacher and student and pastor was forced to interrupt his progress toward a degree until a later day. He said farewell to a lovely group of church members, faculty members and students, and moved away.

Two children were born in the preacher's home while he served in Ewing. Ruth was born October 12, 1912, and Mary was born August 13, 1914.

OTHER EARLY FULL-TIME PASTORATES

The young preacher was never lacking for a place to preach. From the very beginning there was always pulpit committees investigating him and offering him "greener pastures."

First Church, Charleston

Dr. Prince received invitations to visit two churches the day following the meeting of the College Board. He accepted the call of the First Baptist Church of Charleston, Illinois, and moved to that city November 1, 1914. He and his little family spent two very happy years in Charleston. The work in the church prospered, and the fellowship and spirit of the people was all that could be desired. Additions and baptisms occurred frequently. The young pastor was busy with special addresses for family home-comings, lodge services, and other gatherings. Weddings and funerals were numerous.

During this pastorate a monument was placed at the site of the Lincoln-Douglas debate on the fairground at the edge of Charleston. The young preacher delivered the dedicatory address in the presence of 5,000 people. In May, 1915—fifty years after the close of the Civil War—he preached the memorial sermon for the veterans of the Grand Army of the Republic. There were enough veterans present to fill half the space in his church building. All of these have long since answered the final roll call.

First Church, LaGrange

During his second year at Charleston, the First Baptist Church, LaGrange, Missouri, called him three times as pastor. He declined the first and second calls but accepted the third call and moved to LaGrange in September, 1916, immediately enrolling in LaGrange College as he started his work as pastor of the church. He remained there two and one-half years, and graduated from the College in May, 1918. His fourth daughter, Grace, was born there, on January 10, 1917.*

---

* It was common occurrence, on Sunday noon, to see Dr. Prince, jug in hand, walking through LaGrange meditating on the sermon he had just delivered, on his way to the spring on the riverside to fill his jug with mineral water for Sunday lunch. The water was proven to possess certain healthful ingredients and he was a heavy drinker of the mineral water. He was known in LaGrange as a jug-toting preacher—almost a daily exercise for him.

In 1917, when the first draft call was issued under the Selective Service system of the United States Government, he was called for examination and induction into the Army. He passed the examination but was rejected for service because he was a theological student, a pastor, and the father of four children. He was told by the Board of Examiners to go home and find other ways to help in the war effort. He was later assigned the task as Director of Four Minute Speakers, in the Department of Publicity of the United States Government, for Northeast Missouri, and served until he was discharged in February, following the close of the war in November.*

During the pastorate at LaGrange, Dr. S. M. Brown, editor of the Word and Way, the Baptist State paper of Missouri, held a forceful revival in the LaGrange church. This was a red letter event in the church work there. There were a number of ministerial students in the college at that time and these have continued to be life-long friends of Dr. Prince. Most of them have gone now to the Father's house on high.

First Church, Eldorado

In February, 1919, Dr. Prince was called to the pastorate of three churches in the same week. The First Church, Charleston called him to return as pastor there; and he was also called by the Second Baptist Church, Indianapolis, Indiana; and the First Baptist Church of Eldorado, Illinois. He accepted the call to Eldorado, and the family moved to Eldorado in February, 1919, for one of the most happy and fruitful pastorates

* The Four Minute Speakers were directed to speak at every gathering to which they could gain admittance, such as clubs, lodges, theatres, and sometimes in churches. They were supplied with live information from the Government concerning the war effort at all times and relayed this to the people. They spoke four minutes on each occasion.

of his earlier ministry.* Additions were numerous, baptisms frequent, and a happy pastor and people carried out a very fine program. He held some outstanding revivals with this church, not only while pastor but over a span of a quarter of a century. In all, he held ten revivals in this church and in some of these meetings there were one hundred additions, mostly for baptism. His last one was held in February, 1948, while Dr. Herman Moore was pastor there.

One of his best revivals in Eldorado was held in January, 1920. Dr. Julian Atwood, pastor of the First Baptist Church of Marion, Illinois, was the evangelist, and Gospel singer, David M. Hughes of Newport, Kentucky led the singing. The revival continued two weeks and there were more than 100 additions, nearly all of these by baptism. One unique feature of this meeting was the frequency of baptismal services. Two revival services were held daily—at 2:00 p.m. and 7:00 p.m.—and the ordinance of baptism was administered at every service during the revival.**

During the pastorate in Eldorado his fifth daughter, Dorothy Elizabeth, was born March 31, 1921. She is now and has been for years the Curriculum Coordinator for Elementary Schools in Ector County, Odessa, Texas, and is also an author, having recently published her first book. She is a nationally known

---

* Dr. Prince arrived in Eldorado in the midst of the great flu epidemic of 1918-1920. His oldest daughter was ill of flu and pneumonia on his arrival there. Every home was involved in this epidemic. People were dying in large numbers, and at times there were as many as ten funerals in a day. The leading physician of the city came down with the flu, every available nurse in the area was ill at the same time, and the only mortician in Eldorado was also ill. Dr. Prince went day and night, visiting patients and reporting to the doctor to secure medicine for them. He treated the patients, prepared bodies for burial, preached the funeral and served both as preacher and undertaker at the funerals. He often preached the funeral sermon in a room in homes where three or four others were so seriously ill that it was doubtful if they could live through the service, but they wanted to attend the funeral of their loved one.

** Dr. Prince held more revivals for Dr. Atwood than for any other man in his ministry and Dr. Atwood held more revivals for Dr. Prince than any other man. Their love and friendship for each other was similar to that of David and Jonathan. Dr. Prince also used David M. Hughes in more revivals than any other Gospel Singer who ever worked with him.

educator, and is called to speak at educational meetings from coast to coast. She recently received a citation for meritorious service in the field of Education from the University of Missouri, of which she is a graduate.

During this pastorate at Eldorado, Dr. Prince had the unusual privilege of performing the ceremony for the second marriage of his mother, three years after his father passed away. This marriage occurred in Aledo, Illinois, on December 17, 1919, when his mother became the wife of Mr. J. M. Sager.

FIRST CHURCH, MARION, ILLINOIS

During Dr. Prince's last year at Eldorado, the First Baptist Church, Marion, Illinois, twice called him as pastor. The first call was extended in March, 1921, and the second call about six months later. In each case the vote in the Marion Church was taken at the Sunday evening service with large congregations present, and the vote was unanimous. Dr. Prince declined the first call and remained at Eldorado. Thereupon, some business men of Eldorado appeared before the Eldorado Church and told the members that if the church would increase his salary these business men would buy him a new car. Conditions were met immediately and the car was bought by unsaved business men who were not members of the church but who attended Sunday night services regularly. But when the second call came six months later, the young pastor felt that this was surely of the Lord, and so bade farewell to his people at Eldorado and moved to Marion. He refused to take the car with him because he felt it was bought for use in the Eldorado field.

Early in this pastorate, the church put on a Sunday school enlargement campaign. This was done with the able assistance of the heads of departments of the Sunday School Board, Nashville, Tennessee, led by Harold Ingraham and Arthur

Flake. The results were very beneficial to the Sunday school in particular and the work of the church in general. The Sunday school passed the 700 mark in attendance. The Agoga Class, taught by the pastor, moved into a downtown theater; and its enrollment grew to more than 300, and the average attendance above 200 week by week.

Another example of the progress of the Sunday school may be seen in the development and growth of one class for women. After a church census of the community had been taken a list of names of women was given to Mrs. Milan Motsinger, wife of one of the deacons and daughter of Rev. H. C. Mitchell, an outstanding preacher of the preceding generation in Southern Illinois and in the metropolitan St. Louis area. Mrs. Motsinger was assigned a classroom and encouraged to see what she could do toward building a class. She began with only one member and continued to work until she had a class of almost one hundred members, many of whom were not Christians. Most of them were won to Christ and baptized into the fellowship of the church during a revival that broke out one Sunday and continued for three weeks.

Miss Beulah Doerr

This history would not be complete without mention of Miss Beulah Doerr and of all her work as she served with Dr. Prince in the churches and colleges, and with Dr. W. R. White, as youth director, in the great Broadway Baptist Church, Ft. Worth. To write fully of her work would require another book. This nobly gifted woman began work as Director of Music and Education when such workers were very scarce in the Southern Baptist Convention. She was uniformly successful in her work at all places where she served. Her devoted Christian life, and consecration to her task, along with her charming personality was a blessing to hundreds of young people, as well as older people, wherever she went.

When Dr. Prince became pastor at Marion First, he was told that his first assignment would be to find a Director of Music and Education. He did not know where to turn for such help. While he was struggling with the problem, Dr. W. P. Throgmorton told him that there was a young woman, just out of school, who had recently returned to her home at Johnston City, Illinois, five miles north of Marion. Dr. Prince called her by phone and asked her to come to meet the Committee and discuss the work in Marion. A few days later Marion First Church extended her a call. The blessing of the Lord was upon her work from the beginning.

The great growth in the Sunday School, mentioned above, was a result of her leadership. The music department was greatly enlarged. She began Vacation Bible School work before Southern Baptists published literature and books on Bible School work. She worked up her own material and conducted successful schools each year.

When the Prince family moved to Brownwood, Texas, Miss Doerr and her father and mother, and her sister and husband, all moved to Brownwood, where Miss Doerr had been called by the First Baptist Church as Director of Music and Education. She did a marvelous work there over a period of seven years. She went from Brownwood to Broadway Baptist Church in Ft. Worth as Youth Leader during Dr. White's pastorate there.

All in all, she served in one church in Illinois, two in Texas, two in Louisiana, and one in Missouri, serving with remarkable success on every field. She was a skillful educational worker before our seminaries offered many courses in this field. She was a competent Music director and organist, church visitor and general church worker.

Her sister was secretary to Dr. Prince and her father a faithful custodian when Dr. Prince went to Hannibal-LaGrange College. Dr. Prince states that words cannot tell how much the Doerr family meant to him and his family, and to the Lord's work. All of these good people have gone to be with the Lord now except Miss Beulah who has served for a quarter of a century as Dean of Women and Professor of Modern Languages in Hannibal-LaGrange College. During her years in Hannibal she has served as organist and Director of Music in Calvary Baptist Church of Hannibal. Her reward in heaven will be great. God has used her dedicated life in a wonderful way.

Marion, county seat of "bloody" Williamson County, was a troubled spot during the 1920's, and the militant pastor was very active in a clean-up campaign which was participated in vigorously by most of the preachers in the county. On one occasion a truck was backed up under the windows of the sheriff's office and the preachers made speeches scoring the laxity of certain law-enforcement officers, especially the sheriff, who was accused of favoring the lawbreakers. One day twenty-one men were killed in a fracas that developed during a coal miners' strike. Two armed camps formed—one in the east side of the county and the other in the west—and men were roving at large, seeking to kill one another. Almost every man in the county was carrying a gun, and no one was secure. In all the uproar, the county officials were doing nothing. Large crowds thronged the churches at services in which the preachers lashed out against the spineless officials. In retaliation, the lawbreakers set a certain night when they would assassinate every preacher and several other outstanding citizens who had had the courage to raise their voices. A list was made, and various ones of their number were assigned the names of preachers and others whom they were to murder before dawn. But by devious means, the plot became known; precautions were taken, and wholesale slaughter was averted. But this breathtaking escape did not settle the matter. Glenn Young, a U. S. Government officer, was brought in to try to restore order, but he was shot to death one night. A little later, State Patrolman Lory Price, stationed at Marion, was kidnapped along with his wife, and both were shot and killed. His funeral, conducted by Pastor Prince in the First Baptist Church, drew both the concerned and the curious by the hundreds from near and far. The church was heavily guarded—even to the extent of machine guns mounted on the roof—both while the body was lying in state and during the funeral service because of the real or imagined possibility that violence might break out on the spot. The body of Mrs. Price, concealed in an old mine shaft, was not recovered until several months later.

The only hope to improve the situation lay in the election of officers who would enforce the law, and a great campaign was started with this end in mind. One of the elections was a wet and dry campaign in which all the dry candidates were members of the First Baptist Church. The pastors of the First Christian Church and the First Baptist Church were especially active in this campaign. The vote was tabulated and results became known about three o'clock the morning following the election day. All the dry candidates had won, and all were members of the First Baptist Church. Within thirty minutes after the vote was announced, the building of the First Baptist Church was bombed and serious damage was done to the front entrance; the house of worship of the First Christian Church was bombed later. Pastor Prince was away in a revival with the First Church,

Dr. Prince and his family at Marion, Illinois. Left to right: Dorothy, Dr. Prince, Mrs. Prince, "Junior," and Grace. Back row, left to right Ruth, Esther, and Mary.

Eldorado, at the time of the bombing. The rumor went around later that, had he been at home, the men who threw the bomb from the speeding car intended to hurl it into the narrow passageway between the church and the parsonage in hopes of leaving the visible evidence of their vengeance on preacher as well as church.

There was never a dull moment in the Marion First pastorate. Additions and baptisms were the usual order of the day, and the pastor was frequently in revivals in other churches. The congregations were large at all services both in summer and winter. The historian of Marion First Church says that Dr. Prince preached to the largest crowds ever to hear any pastor during the history of the church. The parsonage building mentioned above was erected next door to the church, and the pastor and his family moved into the new home on February 29, 1924. In this home the sixth and last child of the pastor and Mrs. Prince was born on May 23, 1926—the first and only son—A. E. Prince, Jr. He is now employed by Mr. E. G. Rodman, Odessa, Texas, as controller of the companies he owns and operates, and is a Commander, United States Naval Reserve, Retired.

The Marion pastorate closed on Sunday, June 5, 1927. The preacher's resignation was unanimously refused when presented to the church. But feeling the leading of the Spirit to which he had always been attentive, he announced, at a later date that he was leaving anyway; and thus what had been a most pleasant and fruitful pastorate came to a close.

The decade following World War I was a fertile time in church work among Baptists. The Seventy-five Million Campaign had been launched in 1919, and the churches were "calling out the called"—young people volunteering for Christian service—under the leadership of Dr. L. R. Scarborough, President of Southwestern Baptist Seminary and southwide director of the Seventy-five Million Campaign. God was in the midst of his people and there was a distinct "sound of a going in the tops of the mulberry trees." Many felt that the War had truly ended all wars; the Eighteenth Amendment to the Constitution had recently been adopted; the nation had a soul; moral standards were high. It was a great time to be alive and working for God.

Dr. Prince, at age 40, when he began his pastorate at First Baptist Church, Brownwood, Texas. He gave consent for this picture to be used to show that he has not always looked as he looks now.

Men's Bible class — "Line Riders" — First Baptist Church, Brownwood, Texas.

V.

PREACHING IN THE SOUTH

In the late winter of 1927, while trying to recuperate from a stubborn case of influenza, Dr. Prince was advised by his physician to go for a month to a dry, hot climate. At this same time—providentially, it seemed—there came an invitation for him to supply for a month at the First Baptist Church of Brownwood, Texas, in the warm dry heart of the Lone Star State. This was before the day of miracle drugs, and sometimes the only cure for winter-time ailments seemed to be a change of climate. Pale and weak, the preacher boarded the train and alighted a day later in dazzling Texas sunlight. From the first church service onward, the congregation of this pastorless church began to press him on the matter of becoming their pastor; and he—deeply involved in the work of the Marion church and of the Illinois Baptist State Association—had no such notions! The tempo of the pressure was increased day by day. After the second Sunday—disregarding what wonders the Texas sun might possibly have worked upon him had he stayed out the month—he climbed back on the train and headed for home. In the services at the Brownwood church, he had heard for the first time the singing of the hymn, "I shall not be, I shall not be moved," and he said later that all the way home the wheels of the train went round and round to that tune as he supplied the words! His mind was made up. He would stay in Marion!

FIRST CHURCH, BROWNWOOD

But time proved him wrong. He had hardly reached home when a telegram came from Dr. E. Godbold, President of Howard Payne College and chairman of the pulpit committee of the Brownwood church, advising him that upon the recommendation of the pulpit committee, the church had extended him a unanimous call. Just here is an inspiring display of the marvels of Divine leadership in the life of a praying servant of God. Telegrams and letters from members of the Brownwood church, city and state officials, Baptist headquarters, and yet others, poured into the study of the Marion pastor. A committee from the Brownwood church was sent to the Southern Baptist Convention at Louisville, Kentucky, to urge him to accept the call. The sounds of the wheels of the train chanting, "I Shall Not Be Moved," grew weaker and weaker, and the forty year old pastor bade farewell to the congregation of Marion First Church and moved to the heart of the Lone Star State, approximately one thousand miles away.

Brownwood was a thriving city, and the First Baptist Church, sharing the general prosperity, had just finished erecting a new building. The people of the church and of the city gave the new pastor and his family a real Texas welcome. The church provided a stately and commodious home for the pastor and his family until arrangements could be completed for the purchase of a beautiful parsonage next door to the church building.

There were twenty additions to the church at his first service on Sunday morning, June 12, 1927, and seldom a service without additions during the next seven years. The Brownwood pastorate was like the Marion pastorate. Great crowds thronged the Baptist church services and additions were the order of the day at almost every service. A total of about 1,700 people united with the church during the seven years.*

Fourteen revivals were held during this pastorate, and the pastor did the preaching in seven of these revivals. He was assisted in the other revivals by Dr. Frank Weedon, Dr. J. Howard Williams, Dr. Harvey Andrew, Dr. W. R. White, Dr. W. W. Chancellor, Dr. Harlan J. Matthews and Dr. Julian Atwood, seven great Texas Baptist preachers; and in September, 1933, a great association-wide tent revival was held on the campus of the college with Dr. M. E. Dodd as evangelist and William E. Young as singer.

Howard Payne College, the largest Baptist co-educational college in the South, was directly across the street in front of the First Baptist Church. Hundreds of students went through the college during his pastorate. There was an unusually large number of ministerial students, along with a large number of other ministers, active and retired, who held membership in the church—at times as many as two hundred. The First Church pastor was in reality a pastor of pastors. He was their pastor, companion, friend and helper at all times, and spent many hours in conferences with them individually. He also gave lectures to the ministerial students in classes assembled in the college from time to time.

He was also very busy in denominational work. He served for three years as District Leader in District Sixteen in the heart of Texas, having nine associations in this district. So successful was he in this work that he was later asked to assist in setting up district missionaries in the districts throughout

* There was a great urgency about Dr. Prince's work in Brownwood. Perhaps a hint of it appears in the feeling he was heard to express on occasion. One of his daughters recalls how, after church on Sunday nights, as he waited for the family to assemble for their evening prayer together, he would often pace slowly up and down the long living-room saying aloud, "One more Sunday gone. One Sunday nearer Home. One less Sunday to preach the Gospel here on earth."

Texas. He retired from his pastorate at the end of the seventh year and served for a while as assistant to Dr. J. Howard Williams, Executive Secretary for the Baptists of Texas. When all other districts were supplied with missionaries he took the position as the first District Missionary of the Dallas District, the largest Baptist mission district in the world, having at that time eighty-five thousand members.

Dr. Prince and his family moved to Dallas and placed their membership in the First Baptist Church where Dr. George W. Truett was pastor. One of the great experiences of his life was his fellowship with this great man. When Dr. Truett was elected President of the Baptist World Alliance at the meeting of that organization in Berlin, Germany, in 1934, it was Dr. Prince's privilege to preach in his stead in the First Baptist Church, Dallas. He regards this experience as one of the highest in his ministry.*

As usual, Dr. Prince was very busy in revivals in other churches. Here is a list of the names of some of the places where he held revivals while he was pastor in Brownwood: Melvin (2), Mullen, Meridian, Lake Victor, Zephyr, Cross-Cut, West, Brookesmith, Stephenville First, Jordan Springs, Jacksonville, DeLeon, Marshall First, Sulphur Springs, Edgewood, and Canton in Texas; Eldorado (2) and West Frankfort (2) in Illinois; Roswell (2), New Mexico; and Queensborough, Shreveport, Louisiana. He was also the Assembly pastor at

---

* The friendship of Dr. Truett and Dr. Prince continued until Dr. Truett went to be with the Lord. The last time they met was at a state rally of Missouri Baptists at Sedalia, Missouri, in 1942, where they spoke from the same platform in one of the services. His heart has ever been humbled and prompted to the deepest gratitude by an incident that happened there. Dr. Truett was the featured speaker for the three-day conference and delivered an address at each service. It was a bitterly cold week, and the snow was about six inches deep. Dr. Truett did not usually come for the early part of the service since he was always to bring the closing message. On the night Dr. Prince was to speak, Dr. Truett came down early into the hotel lobby, and when some one expressed surprise that he was starting so early to the church, he said: "I am going to hear Prince." Dr. Prince says the fact that so great a man would take the trouble to hear him is a cause for humility of the greatest degree and that no greater tribute was ever given to him.

Baptist Hill in Missouri, and Baptist Assembly, Menard, Texas, and delivered addresses at several other assemblies.

During the Brownwood pastorate two of the pastor's daughters were married in large church weddings. Ruth became the wife of Mr. Allen Hunt of Kerrville, Texas, on August 25, 1931. Esther was married to Mr. Howard L. Jackson of Brownwood on April 13, 1934. All four had been students at Howard Payne College. Today Howard is an accountant and Esther a legal secretary in Fort Worth, Texas. Ruth is employed in the post office at Kerrville. Allen, a long-time postal employee, passed away on April 30, 1961.

PASTOR IN LOUISIANA

The position as District Missionary was far from remunerative. In fact, he found it impossible to live and support his family on the meager salary. Moreover, he had two daughters who should be in college and he could not send them to school on his income. The family had really come to a time of crisis.

One day as he was returning home from a busy day's work as District Missionary, he felt led to pull his car off the main road and give his whole attention to prayer. It was a gracious season of prayer. Somehow as he talked with the Lord, he felt encouraged to describe to the Lord the kind of people he would like to serve as pastor—a people who loved the Lord and were eager to serve Him, a people who were willing to learn and anxious for the welfare of their children, a people who would match pastoral leadership with down-to-earth followship—a people whose love and respect for their pastor was warm and strong and whose tithes and offerings were gratefully given. As he resumed his journey homeward, and reflected on that season of prayer, he felt that this was a rather large order and he had no idea just where such a church could be found, but he felt a definite peace in his heart. He went on home and went soberly but expectantly about his duties as District Missionary.

FIRST CHURCH, PINEVILLE

Within two weeks he received a letter from Dr. H. M. Weatherby, Dean of Louisiana College and chairman of the pulpit committee of the First Church, Pineville, Louisiana, stating that the church was pastorless, that Dr. Prince was under consideration by the committee, and that the church would like for him to come for a visit. He went to Pineville on Sunday, July 22, 1934, and was called as pastor on Sunday night, July 29, 1934. He accepted the call and moved to Pineville as soon as he could close his work as District Missionary. He arrived in Pineville with his family on Thursday, August 30, 1934, and began his pastorate there on Sunday, September 2nd.

The call to Pineville was an answer to his prayer. Dr. Prince says that if ever the Lord led a man to a field, He certainly led him to this field. This church was everything he had envisioned in his roadside prayer.*

The dark days of the depression lingered long in Louisiana, and a large number of the church members found it a struggle to make a living. Many of the men were employed at the Central Louisiana State Hospital adjoining the city and were receiving $32.50 per month. But from their pay checks, a tithe was immediately given to their church. How they ever lived on the remainder is difficult to see. On those rare occasions when

* The family of Dr. Prince has always made much of prayer in the solution of the affairs of the home, the church, and the personal needs of each member of the family. Dr. Prince was busily engaged in his study at the church, one Saturday afternoon. His daughter, Dorothy, was to be in a program at the church on Sunday and she really needed a pair of shoes. She called her father, and said: "Papa, I need a pair of shoes, and if I will pray for you to have a wedding, and my prayer is answered, will you give me the fee to buy a pair of shoes?" Dr. Prince replied: "Certainly, I will." He turned again to his work. A few minutes later a young couple came to the door and asked to be married. The ceremony was performed, and the fee was $5.00, which was exactly the amount needed by Dorothy. She bought her shoes. And she still believes in prayer.

Miss Doerr and her officers and committee of The Youth Week program at First Baptist Church, Pineville, Louisiana. Miss Doerr is standing at right of the "Flam-ing Torch" placard in the picture.

one of them got a raise in salary, he could be seen joyfully making his way to the pastor's study to tear up his old pledge card and to sign a new one, pledging a tithe of his new salary to the church budget.

The church and pastor went forward in a vigorous program of evangelism. Dr. Prince did the preaching in most of the revivals during his pastorate there. There were additions at almost every service, whether or not a revival meeting was in progress. Most of the revivals were for a period of two weeks, with the morning service held at the chapel hour in Louisiana College and evening service in the church. During this pastorate more than 1,500 people came for church membership and hundreds of others were led to a rededication of themselves to Christ. Almost as many more were led to Christ in revivals held by the pastor in other chuches during these years. One of these revivals was held in the First Baptist Church of West Monroe in May, 1938. Pastor E. E. Huntsberry and the deacons presented Dr. Prince the following resolution on the closing night of the revival:

> The pastor and deacons of the First Baptist Church of West Monroe, Louisiana, assembled in special session on the closing night of our great revival, by unanimous vote express our gratitude to our evangelist, Dr. A. E. Prince, for his faithful ministry in our special evangelistic services. We note that there have been 41 additions by letter and 114 for baptism, the largest number ever received in any revival meeting in the history of our church, and that great victories have been won in the hearts and lives of our people. We are unanimously agreed that this is the greatest revival ever held thus far in our church, and the closing Sunday was the greatest Sunday in the history of our church.
>
> E. E. Huntsberry, Pastor
> First Baptist Church
> West Monroe, Louisiana

A revival he held in Highland Park Baptist Church, Texarkana, Texas, this same year was declared to be the greatest revival in the history of that church up to that time.

Other revivals during his pastorate in Pineville were held in Istrouma Baptist Church, Baton Rouge; Poland Baptist Church, Poland, Louisiana; and the First Baptist Churches in Winnfield, Ansley, Chatham, Jena, Tioga, Glenmore, Delhi, Leesville, Homer, Minden, Bunkie, Jonesville, Jonesboro, Pine Grove, Olla, Colfax, Urania, Rochelle and Bentley, Louisiana; Fulton and Vandalia, Missouri; First Baptist Churches in Arkadelphia, Elaine and North Little Rock, Arkansas; DeKalb, Texas; Eldorado and West Frankfort, Illinois, and yet others.

Louisiana College, the Baptist College of Louisiana, is located in Pineville, and two of his daughters finished their college work there. Dr. Claybrook Cottingham was the able president of the college during that time, and Dr. H. M. Weathersby was dean. There was a strong faculty and an active student body.*

He took an active part in the program of training in the church, teaching many books in the study courses and fostering an active program of Bible study and the reading of uplifting books. He started a "Book of the Month" club for his congregation. A book was selected each month and these were purchased by the people, read during that month, and then placed in their libraries at home. This plan proved to be quite popular with the people.

His efforts were a challenge to many, and the people responded and grew.

* Although Dr. Prince has always been a tender shepherd to his people whereever he had been, it seems in retrospect that the pastoral side of his nature reached full maturity in these years at Pineville. His compassion for his people when they were in trouble or sorrow knew no limits. He was indefatigable—finding ever more and more ways to be of service to them. Any midnight or any dawn might find him hurrying into Baptist Hospital in Alexandria in answer to some anguished telephone call. Always he made himself available—to the person exhuberant over good news, to the person who wanted to pray, to the person who wanted advice from one in whom he could safely confide.

His daughter, Grace, was married November 22, 1938, in a lovely church wedding in the First Baptist Church, Pineville, to Dr. Glen Lee Greene, now pastor of the First Baptist Church, Oak Ridge, Louisiana, and historian for the Louisiana Baptist Convention. Grace is now a teacher in Oak Ridge public schools.

TWO GREAT REVIVALS

Two of the outstanding revivals of his ministry were held during his pastorate at Pineville. These were real revivals with great demonstration of the power of God in the churches. Both revivals were in college towns. Probably as many as 500 people marked definite changes in their lives from each of these meetings.

Pineville's Great Revival

A revival broke out in Pineville, and Louisiana College in the spring of 1935. The opening Sunday began with a sunrise prayer meeting attended by more than 400 people, and was a great day with mighty demonstrations of the power of God. This meeting continued 16 days, with the pastor preaching and Rev. A. E. Pardue leading the singing. The college, the church, and all of Central Louisiana was shaken by the power of God. The morning services in the College Chapel were wonderful in the impact made on the young people attending the college. The church building was crowded at night, many people standing throughout the time of the service. More than 250 people were reached in that revival, and about 40 of the converts were church members. It was one of the greatest revivals ever in the college and in the church.* The pastor baptized 78 on

* When assessing the various contributions to the success of the Spirit-led revival in Pineville, one must not omit a daily prayer meeting held by the ministerial students of Louisiana College. These young ministers met daily with Dr. Prince, Monday through Friday, in a prayer room at the First Baptist Church to pray for a revival. Dr. Prince taught a book on prayer and gracious seasons of prayer followed the lesson at each meeting.

the closing night of the meeting which is the largest number ever baptized by him at one time. Others were baptized on the following Sundays for some time. The pastor's son, A. E. Prince, Jr., was baptized on that closing night of the revival. Even to this day Dr. Prince gets letters from students of those days in Pineville telling how the influence of that revival still shapes and inspires their lives.

Revival in Arkadelphia, Arkansas

Early in 1937, Dr. Prince was invited to hold a revival in Arkadelphia, Arkansas. The First Baptist Church and Ouachita College jointly sponsored the meeting. He arrived in Arkadelphia on Monday, February 22, 1937, for a fifteen day meeting. The college chapel service was joined with the morning service at the church, and all evening services were in the church. This was a wonderful season of revival with more than 250 definite decisions for Christ. The whole city was shaken by the revival. The meeting was such a pervading demonstration of the power of God that people lodging in the hotel over night felt the impact of the revival atmosphere. Dr. J. R. Grant, President of the college, was very influential in the meeting. The First Church was pastorless at that time, due to the death of Dr. H. L. Winburn, who had served the church for many years.

A continuous prayer meeting was held twenty-four hours a day from the opening day to the close of the revival. The whole city and the regions around knew that some person or persons were praying every minute of every day. The continuous prayer service was spontaneous and voluntary, arranged without any previous plans. Many other prayer meetings were held in the dormitories at the college and in homes in the city. Dr. O. W. Yates, head of the Bible Department, and Dr. Ralph C. Daily, head of the History Department, both rendered much helpful service during the revival.

Dr. Prince spent the afternoons each school day at the college in conference with students. A secretary was assigned to guide the traffic of students to his office. Many mountain-top experiences came in these conferences. The meeting gained momentum day by day. During the second week he had the privilege of leading to Christ the waitress who was assigned to serve his meals in the hotel dining room, and she was baptized on the closing night of the revival. Many of the ministerial students and missionary volunteers who participated have since gone to the ends of the earth carrying the impact of that revival. Dr. Prince says it was wonderful to be there and to witness what transpired hour by hour.

At the closing service Sunday night, March 7, 1937, after baptizing a number of converts, he preached and gave the invitation. People came down every aisle. The altar was crowded with people and still they came until he had to leave to catch his train for home about 9:30 p.m. The revival was still going on when he left the auditorium by a side door. How much we all long to see another such revival! When God's people work and pray, victories are won.

He was unanimously called as pastor of this church after the revival but was not led to accept. Dr. Grant was chairman of the Pulpit Committee.

A Great Funeral Service

One of the most remarkable funeral services of Dr. Prince's ministry was held in the First Baptist Church, Pineville, on Friday, May 31, 1935. The Sunday School Superintendent, Mr. C. W. Brister, had been crushed by a truck some ten days before and had passed away. He was a man about 40 years of age and was loved and respected by everyone. The service was held at 9:45 a.m., which was the Sunday School hour, except that the funeral was on Friday. The church building was crowded to capacity, with people standing around the walls on both main floor and balcony as well as in the vestibule and in the church yard all around the building.

A State Sunday School Convention was in progress at Louisiana College that week with several of the departmental workers of the Baptist Sunday School Board participating in the program. The convention adjourned for the funeral and these denominational leaders stood with others around the walls. Rev. A. E. Pardue was soloist and at the close of the service he sang "Sunrise Tomorrow" in his own inimitable way. It was an hour never to be forgotten.

Mrs. Brister had requested that at the close of the program the pastor should stand beside the casket and extend an invitation to unsaved people to come to Christ, and to back-sliders to return to God. Brother Pardue sang an invitation hymn and fifteen people came down the aisles with tear-stained faces in response to the invitation. The power of the Lord was present to heal in that service. During the next few days Dr. Prince had letters from all the Sunday School Board workers stating that never had they seen such a service.

One thing that impressed the pastor greatly was the fact that two days later, Mrs. Brister and her little son and daughter were present for the church service singing with the rest of the Sunday morning congregation. The son, Dr. C. W. Brister, Jr., became a minister and is now a teacher in Southwestern Baptist Seminary. Dr. Prince says he can never tell them how much this total experience blessed his poor life, and no one will ever know the full effect of it all until the last wave of time has washed the shores of eternity.

DENOMINATIONAL WORK

Mention has already been made of the work Dr. Prince did

for his denomination in Texas. His assignments took him to every part of the Lone Star State. He continued to render service for the Baptist work on his removal to Louisiana on even a larger scale.

The Louisiana Baptist Convention met in Shreveport First Church November 18-22, 1935. Dr. Prince was elected to membership on the State Board, and delivered four addresses to the convention, speaking on the *"Prove-Me Plan," State Missions,* the *Baptist Book Store,* and *Christian Education.* When Pineville First Church and Louisiana College jointly were hosts to the convention at the 1936 annual meeting he was elected president of the Executive Board of the Convention—a position he held until he left the state five years later. As president of the Board, he was ex-officio member of every committee and this responsibility required many miles of travel to various meetings. Mr. F. J. Katz had long been the honored Executive Secretary of Louisiana Baptists. During his last year in office he was kept close to home by the illness of his wife and the Pineville pastor did much of the work for the secretary that year. He served two years as publicity director of the Louisiana Baptist Convention during this time and was a member of the Board of the Louisiana Baptist Hospital in Alexandria all the while he served in the state.

During these five years he had many weddings and funerals and delivered commencement addresses and various other special addresses on many occasions. He was in revival meetings much of the time. He served as Chaplain of the U. S. Veterans Hospital, the State Hospital for the Insane, the State Industrial School for Girls, all at Pineville, and for the Louisiana Baptist Hospital in Alexandria all at the same time and still carried on his work as pastor. He preached five times on Sunday when in the city. His was a "heap strenuous life." This was the aftermath of the great depression, and times were still hard in Pineville, but he was busy and exceedingly happy.

FIRST CHURCH, WEST MONROE

On January 28, 1939, in the First Baptist Church of West Monroe, Dr. Prince preached the funeral of Pastor E. E. Huntsberry. He had died suddenly of a heart attack. The church building was filled to overflowing. Many pastors from all over the state were present for the service. The body was taken to Beaumont, Texas, for burial. Brother Huntsberry had been one of the best of Louisiana pastors.

A short time later, faced with the responsibility of finding a new pastor, the pulpit committee of this church, with unanimous vote, requested Dr. Prince to consider their request to be permitted to place his name before the church. A large number of the members came to Pineville to urge him to take the West Monroe Church. After much prayerful consideration he was called and finally accepted the call and began his pastorate there on Sunday, April 2, 1939. This was the third largest Baptist Church in Louisiana, with a beautiful building and a wonderful group of people.

One of the first things that happened in his pastorate there was the marriage of his daughter, Mary, to Dr. Edwin F. Moore on May 28, 1939, in a beautiful church wedding. The people were very gracious and kind to the preacher's family on this occasion. Mary, formerly Professor of Education at Hannibal-LaGrange College, has been for several years Professor of English at Baylor University. Dr. Moore, formerly Dean of Hannibal-LaGrange College, and later on the faculty of Baylor University, is now a Research Specialist in Rocketdyne Solid Rocket Division of the North American Aviation, Inc. at Waco, Texas.

Dr. Prince was still president of the State Board, and a member of all committees. He was also carrying some of the

Congregation at Sunday morning service, First Baptist Church, West Monroe, Louisiana, taken just before the sermon by Dr. Prince.

First Baptist Church, West Monroe, and parsonage at left of church building. This building has been demolished and the church owns a whole city block and has a church plant which covers most of that space.

load for Secretary Katz. He was as busy as ever.

Twice Host of Louisiana Convention

An unusual thing occurred at this point. With Dr. Prince as host pastor, the Louisiana Baptist Convention met with his church in Pineville in 1938 and at the close of its session it voted to meet in West Monroe in 1939. Dr. Prince moved during the year and was host to the Convention in West Monroe at the next annual Convention. Surely this kind of situation has seldom been paralleled!

In the West Monroe Church he continued his usual evangelistic program. He had had a radio Sunday School program at Pineville for three years and continued it on the station at Monroe, speaking thirty minutes each Saturday morning on the Sunday School lesson for the next day. The largest budget in the history of the church was made up, and it was fully subscribed in one Sunday afternoon at an Open House held by the church. This was the turning point in the financial affairs of that church, and growth in every department followed. Additions to the church were the rule on Sundays, and baptisms were frequent, 49 converts being baptized in a single service at the close of one Spirit-led revival. Dr. Prince did the preaching in all the revivals during his pastorate in West Monroe, and continued to hold revivals in other churches. This was a very happy pastorate and it was his expectation to remain in it for years, for he saw many possibilities in the West Monroe field. But a surprise was in store for him. His old college called for his services. A committee from the college called on him in the summer of 1940 asking him to consider the presidency of the college at Hannibal, Missouri, but at that time he did not feel led to leave his pastorate. The request was renewed one year later, and he finally turned his back on another very pleasant pastorate and moved to Missouri.

VI.

COLLEGE PRESIDENT

One turn as college president is enough for any man, but Dr. Prince has been guilty of trying this three times. He says this may explain why he looks as he does today! He says he has to find some excuse for his appearance.

Ewing College

His first experience as college president was in Ewing College. He was the tenth and last president of Ewing College. On July 10, 1924, at the meeting of the Board of Directors of the Illinois Baptist State Association, he was unanimously elected to the office of president over his vigorous protest against such action. No school was ever so dear to his heart as old Ewing. It was the first college he ever attended and he lacked only a few hours of graduating from the college in 1915.

As has been stated in an earlier chapter of this book, the Board of Trustees of the college wanted to elect him to the office of president when Dr. William A. Matthews left the college in 1912. He refused to be elected in 1912, but was given the power of president and told to do the work while the Board sought for a man. He had to secure a faculty, enlist students, publish a catalog, serve as registrar, while serving as pastor of the First Baptist Church. It was a long, hot and dry summer. He was not an experienced school man at that time, but he did find a new faculty, and had 150 students enrolled in September. This was an unusually good year for the college.

Ewing College Library building — the last of the buildings on the campus to be demolished. The officers of the Alumni Association (1960) are (left to right) President Prince, M. C. Ingram, Mrs. Lorene Wingo, Rev. Kenneth Hall, Dr. Russell Wallis, and Rev. H. E. Lockard.

Ewing College Alumni Association meeting, 1961. Dr. Prince is president of the Association and meetings are held annually on the first Saturday in October. The house of worship of First Baptist Church, Ewing, is in background.

He was also host to the preachers and others who attended the Throgmorton-Daily debate in the College Chapel in the summer of 1912, along with all the other work he had to do. Ewing College was at an all time low, and it was an up-hill job to carry on. Dr. E. L. Carr was chosen president and came to office at the beginning of the fall term. Dr. Prince served with him in the college until that dark day in October in 1914, when the Board of Trustees advised the faculty to look elsewhere for positions because there was no money to pay the employees. He left the college in November of that year, and so terminated his first round of chores as college president, registrar, student, teacher and college pastor.

All of this was an orientation program for Dr. Prince and a preparation for presidential work later on. His term as president of Ewing College in 1924-25 was short and not very impressive. Most of Illinois Baptist people had given up all hope of saving the school.

He was a very busy pastor at that time at Marion First Church and could not give up his pastorate because there was no money to pay his salary at Ewing. He had to keep his church. Prof. August Griesel, who was Acting President before the election of Dr. Prince, took the office of dean and carried on the school on the campus while Dr. Prince travelled in behalf of the college. It was a thankless task. The Board of Directors of the Illinois Baptist State Association met at Ewing in July, 1925, and, after a long session and much discussion, voted to close the college. The last president went home a broken-hearted man. So much for his first presidential chores.

There is a postscript that should be added here. A group of graduates, former students, former Board members and teachers met in Ewing on October 2, 1959, and did something that probably was never done before in the history of the world when they formed an Alumni Association thirty-three years after the College was closed. Dr. Prince was elected president of that Alumni Association and has served since that day to the present time. The Association meets annually on the first Saturday in October each year in the First Baptist Church of Ewing, Illinois. At the first meeting, October 2, 1959, the president was asked to write a history of Ewing College, and he wrote and printed the book, which was released at the annual reunion in 1961.

Four years ago the Association took steps to erect a memorial monument on the first acre of land ever given for the purpose of establishing Ewing College. This land was given by William A. King, one of the founders of Ewing College and lies directly across the street in front of the Ewing Bank. A beautiful monument was dedicated at the annual reunion three years ago. Judge W. Joe Hill delivered a great address at the dedication. The reunion continues to be held annually, and plans are now under way for a great Centennial celebration of the founding of Ewing College on the first Saturday in October, 1967.

Hannibal-LaGrange College

Dr. Prince's second round as college president began with his election to the presidency of his old college—now known as Hannibal-LaGrange College, Hannibal, Missouri, on April 21, 1941. Mention has already been made of the fact that he left a most happy pastorate at West Monroe, Louisiana, to accept this call. This was one of the greatest ventures of faith he has ever made.

The college owed approximately $200,000, most of it bonded indebtedness. The creditors had started foreclosure proceedings. The legal notices were to be posted on the doors of the buildings on September 5, 1941. The Baptists of Missouri had given up all hope of saving the college. Dr. Prince conducted a financial campaign all summer seeking to find money to take up the bonds. Another religious group wanted to buy the college and would have paid the debt and have taken possession on September 5th, had he failed. It was a man-killing and soul-crushing job. On September 5th he took the money to the bank in St. Louis just at the last minute and saved the college for the Baptists.

But for the grace of God, and the selfless sacrifice of the newly-elected president this great school would have been lost to Missouri Baptists. The sacrifices and sufferings, long days and sleepless nights on the part of the president are neither remembered nor mentioned now, but the fact remains that God was with him when all others failed. There was a Board of Trustees that stood by him from his first day as president until he drove out of the campus gate almost ten years later. They never failed him. They were right on the field and knew all of his suffering and hardship to save the school.

He took up the bonds on Friday, September 5, 1941, and set about to open the college the following Tuesday. He telephoned all over the United States to secure a faculty and had a faculty on hand Tuesday to help open the school. Four of these held Ph.D. degrees and others master's degrees. Forty students were enrolled for the fall term.

Pearl Harbor was bombed December 7, 1941, and the whole world was plunged into the Second World War. His teachers and most of his boys were called into military service and left the campus. The girls took positions as secretaries, and various other positions, to help win the war. The doors of the college were almost closed. He had to run a flight school for the

Government to keep the doors open. This continued for two years, with new contingents of men arriving every eight weeks. He had to enlist these men in military service and find a new contingent every eight weeks. Only God could bring him through those awful days. The college was never closed. When the war was over the usual college work was resumed and the college grew year by year and reached the largest enrollment ever in its long history up to that time, and graduated the largest classes ever graduated from the school up to that time The college was founded at LaGrange in 1858, and was moved to Hannibal in 1928. He had graduated from the college at LaGrange in 1918. Only God knows what it cost him to be president of his old school. A whole book could be written about the trials and triumphs of the decade he spent there.

The following paragraphs are from the annual report to the Missouri Baptist General Convention a short time before the close of his work with the college, and sets forth some of the things accomplished during his administration:

> On October 13, 1941, President Prince was inaugurated in the presence of a small faculty, approximately forty students, and a very small group of friends. The College was deeply involved in debt at that time and had no financial standing. It had been removed from the list of accredited colleges and had no scholastic standing. The College has made much progress during these years. The gifts to the College for these eight years amount to $287,694.14 and a total of $311,952.69 has been received for tuition and fees. The total of all gifts, tuition and fees for the eight-year period is $599,646.83.
>
> The College has spent thousands of dollars for repairs and equipment during the eight years. The debts have been liquidated and the College was long ago restored to the list of accredited schools. During the past eight years fourteen buildings have been placed on the campus—five apartment buildings, one classroom building, three six-stall garages, two barns, one chicken house, one slaughter house, and a student center building. Two of these buildings have been

erected during the past year—one barn and one duplex apartment building.

During the past eight years the following improvements have been made in addition to what is listed above: The interior of both dormitories redecorated twice and new furniture placed in all rooms of both dormitories; every window in the Administration building and the dormitories stripped with metal window stripping; a deep freeze walk-in unit installed; one 150 cubic foot refrigerator installed in the kitchen; automatic ice making machine installed. the dining room redecorated and fluorescent lights installed; a new Baldwin organ purchased and installed in the College Chapel; 140 lots previously sold by the College years ago as building sites, purchased by the College; a retirement plan for teachers provided; hundreds of dollars worth of equipment added to the several departments, and hundreds of books to the library; the College kitchen completely changed and two large gas ranges added; a large cellar built; a movie projector secured for use in classroom work; two wire recording machines purchased; two Bendix washing machines purchased and installed in the dormitories; two tractors purchased for the farm; two trucks purchased; and various other farm implements. The College has secured approximately $115,000 worth of Government surplus material including $25,000 worth of first grade lumber. All of this has been secured and paid for with current expense funds, and no debts have been incurred.

The arduous task as president could not keep this busy man out of revivals. During his term with the College, he was in fruitful revivals in Fifth Street, Hannibal; First Baptist Church and Oak Street Baptist Church, Burlington, Iowa; Broken Bow, Nebraska; Pine Lawn, Southwest, and Euclid Church, St. Louis; Antioch and Providence Baptist Churches, in Hannibal area; First Church, Boonville, First Church, Troy, and Bales Baptist Church, Kansas City, Missouri; Second Baptist Church, Hopkinsville, Kentucky; Gordon Street, Atlanta, Georgia; First Church, Eldorado, Illinois, Bethel Baptist Church, Denver, Colorado and others.

OTHER PASTORATES IN MISSOURI

It seems to be a fixed principle of the life of Dr. Prince to have not less than two jobs at one time, and he started his work in Hannibal with two positions.

Fifth Street Baptist Church

During the first three years of his tenure as President of the College, he was also Pastor of Fifth Street Baptist Church—the largest evangelical Church in Northeast Missouri. One unusual thing about this pastorate is that he did not receive one cent of salary for the time he served. The regular salary was paid directly to the College and the money used to help needy students. This was done at his request. He had the joy of knowing that all his service there was a service of love. The work at the church moved along in a very satisfactory manner. There were 324 additions to the Church during his pastorate there, a large percent of the additions were by baptism.

By a strange coincidence, Fifth Street Baptist Church began to broadcast the Sunday morning services on his second Sunday as pastor there and this was continued throughout his pastorate and the last broadcast was on his closing Sunday. The duties of the pastorate kept him off the field for college work on Sundays, but through these radio services, he was able each Sunday to preach to the people throughout the territory of the College in Missouri, Iowa and in Illinois. This was a very profitable ministry to a great area.

Two men, students of the College, served as assistant pastor at Fifth Street Church and this was a very helpful service for the busy pastor and president. Rev. Loyd Self served until he graduated from the College, and Rev. Joe Causey succeeded him and served until he graduated and left Hannibal. These young men were greatly loved and appreciated by the people of Fifth Street Church.

Like all his other pastorates, his sojourn with Fifth Street was a very delightful experience. He thanked God every day for the cooperation of those faithful people in that good church. As the College grew, the work as pastor and president became too heavy, and he resigned at the close of his third year. Rev. Fred Pulliam who was called as Assistant Pastor after the student assistants left, was called to succeed him in the pastorate.

By unanimous vote of the Church, Dr. Prince was elected Pastor Emeritus for life on the night his resignation was accepted. Because of this he feels an unusually close relationship to that great Church even to this day.

On Friday, December 13, 1946, regardless of day or date, Miss Betty Threlkeld, daughter of Mr. and Mrs. H. M. Threlkeld, Mexico, Missouri, and the pastor's only son, A. E. Prince, Jr. were married by the groom's father in a lovely church wedding in Fifth Street Baptist Church.

Grassy Creek Baptist Church

Soon after closing his work at Fifth Street Church, he was called to serve at Grassy Creek Baptist Church near Louisiana, Missouri. This was for half-time work. It was a most delightful change to turn his back on the college and drive through the hills to Grassy Creek Church two Sundays each month. The people were uniformly kind and gracious and did so much to make his stay a happy experience. He served there about two years. It was like old times to serve a country church, especially one with such a long and honorable history of service. It was with reluctance that he turned from this lovely church and community.

Immanuel Baptist Church

Following the pastorate at Grassy Creek, he served full time as pastor of Immanuel Baptist Church, Hannibal, Missouri for two years. Immanuel Church had much difficulty in its early years with problems as to location and resources for sustaining the work. The church, at the first, did not have good cooperation of the sister churches and had difficulty in supporting a pastor. The other churches felt that there was not room for another church. These good people were finally successful in getting a good location on Highway 61 at St. Marys Avenue. There was on the lot a building sufficient for their use and it was about this time that Dr. Prince began his work.*

The church has prospered. It is not far from the college campus and a number of fine students and faculty members hold membership in the church and render very helpful service. His fellowship with this good church was very refreshing and the work prospered as the Lord led them forth in the work. Today, Immanuel Church has a new and adequate building and a recently constructed educational building. It is rendering a great service to the fastest growing section of the city.

Dr. Prince has always had a pastor's heart, and throughout all his tenure of office as student, teacher, dean, college president and denominational worker, he has maintained an almost unbroken line of service as pastor. This was true during most of the years he spent in Hannibal.

His chore as principal of a Baptist Academy and his third assignment as college president will be discussed under his work in Hawaii later in this book.

---

* The building secured by Immanuel Church was an erstwhile tavern. These good people rearranged the interior and redecorated the building inside and out, and made of it a very serviceable building for worship services and church activities. It is amazing to note the transformation which takes place when God moves into a building!

LIFE'S GREATEST SORROW

No other man has ever invested as much in Hannibal-LaGrange College as Dr. Prince. His wife worked untiringly by day and night to help him win the battle. She served in many ways and held up his hands while he toiled for the school. She finally became dietitian of the college and served without pay in this capacity for about two years. The work was too much for her. She was stricken with a fatal heart attack on the afternoon of October 17, 1946, and died in Levering Hospital at day-break on the following morning. All that he had ever suffered was as nothing compared to the agony of soul he suffered in this hour. For days and weeks afterward he was broken under the burden of this staggering loss. He was one of the loneliest of men and walked about in a dazed condition for weeks. His was a sorrow that affected every part of his being.

The memorial service was held on Monday, October 21, 1946, 2:30 p.m., in Fifth Street Baptist Church. Dr. Fred McArthur of Central Baptist Church, Quincy; Dr. Maurice Anderson, missionary to China but formerly Bible teacher at Hannibal-LaGrange; Dr. A. Paul Smith, one of Dr. Prince's boys in the ministry; Pastor Fred Pulliam of Fifth Street Church; and Hon. Walter Goodson, president of the Board of Trustees of the college, participated in the service at Fifth Street Baptist Church in the presence of a large congregation. Afterward he and his children stood beside her open grave in beautiful Grand View Cemetery in Hannibal for the closing prayer led by Dr. W. A. Kleckner, of the college faculty. Nightfall closed one of the darkest days of Dr. Prince's life.

Another memorial service was held in the College Chapel a few days later, with Dr. Paul Weber, Jr., as featured speaker.

Commenting on Mrs. Prince's beautiful life of unselfish service for the young people of the college, and how in her strenuous toil, with their welfare ever in mind, she had broken under the ordeal and had fallen asleep, he summed up his message with the statement that Mrs. Prince had died a martyr to the cause of Christian education, and that her name deserved to be listed on the honor roll of the immortal martyrs of the ages.

It was Dr. Prince's intention to leave the college after the loss of his companion who had walked beside him for more than thirty-seven years, but the Board of Trustees met the day after the funeral and asked him to continue with the college. The Trustees started a fund to erect a memorial building on the campus in her memory. Dr. K. J. O'Banion gave the first donation for this building. Mrs. Lillian Pulliam and her children, of loveland, Colorado, who had given to the college from time to time, gave $15,000 to the fund. President Prince was in charge of the drive for funds and the erection of a president's home as a memorial to her. This assignment was completed in 1950 and he left the campus at the opening of the fall term in September.

After President Calvin Coolidge had stood beside the bed in a Washington Hospital and saw his son, Calvin, Jr., pass into death, he said: "The glory of the Presidency departed in that hour." He felt that perhaps if he had never gone to Washington, this might not have happened. On going to Hannibal, Dr. Prince gave up the last home he and Mrs. Prince ever had and lived for almost ten years in some rooms in one of the dormitories. Shall we say that if he had never gone to Hannibal he might have kept his home and his companion? Only God can answer that question for President Coolidge or for Dr. Prince.

"Not now but in the coming years,
It may be in the better land;
We'll know the meaning of our tears,
And then, yes then, we'll understand."

In his annual Christmas message written a few days after her death, he graphically portrayed the attitude and reaction of his soul to his greatest loss. The same Jesus who spoke to his soul when he was but a little lad, and said, "Son, thy sins be forgiven thee," who stood beside him on that dark day when death first came to his childhood home, who stood beside him when sister went away, and when father, and mother, and brothers went away, who hovered near when he lay at the gates of death, now stood by him when he came to the greatest sorrow of his life—the homegoing of the wife of his youth and the mother of his children.

FIRST CHURCH, EFFINGHAM, ILLINOIS

He was a broken man physically and could not go on. He was also almost to compulsory retirement age and could not have served but a brief time. It was a real relief to drive out of the College gate for the last time as school opened for the 1950-51 session and head for Effingham, Illinois, where he had accepted the interim pastorate of the First Baptist Church.

Three years after his companion passed away, he had been married to Miss Faye Dixon, daughter of Mr. and Mrs. William Dixon of New Florence, Missouri. She is well known and greatly loved by the people wherever he has served since the day of their marriage. She has made for him the first home he has had for many years. He cannot say in words all that she has meant and means to him. Together they have borne their griefs and carried their sorrows, and toiled on hopefully, faithfully, prayerfully; and he thanks God for her and her radiant spirit and understanding heart.

Faye Dixon Prince

The people of Effingham received them most cordially, and they made some of life's most cherished friends there. What was intended to be a three month's interim pastorate ran on for twelve months. The Effingham Church is one of the best, and they had most delightful fellowship in the work with the people. There were about 100 additions to the Church, more than half of them by baptism.

He kept up his record for revivals while serving in Effingham. He was in good revivals at First Church, Louisville, Illinois; First Church, Newport, Kentucky; Hill Baptist Church, Augusta, Georgia; and in Mt. Holly, North Carolina. There were approximately 300 additions in these revivals.

One difficulty he has had in interim pastorates has been getting loose. Only one interim pastorate has ever closed on time. The one at Effingham lasted exactly a year. The last service was held on Sunday morning, August 5, 1951. Mr. and Mrs. Kenneth Starkey took him and Mrs. Prince to St. Louis on Sunday afternoon, via Enfield, Illinois, where he assisted in the funeral of his uncle, Edward M. Young. The closing hymn at Effingham was very expressive of the feelings of two people leaving for New Zealand. The chorus was:

"Take up thy cross and follow me,"
I heard my Saviour say;
"I gave my life to ransom thee,
Surrender your all today."

"Wherever He leads, I'll go,
Wherever He leads, I'll go,
I'll follow my Christ who loves me so,
Wherever He leads, I'll go.*

* Copyright 1936 by the Sunday School Board of The Southern Baptist Convention.

VII.

PREACHING BEYOND THE SEA

In July, 1951, Dr. Prince received a letter from the Baptist Tabernacle, Auckland, New Zealand, asking if he could serve as interim pastor of the Tabernacle for six months. This greatest of New Zealand churches had been pastorless for about two years, following a serious division in the church. The church had never had a Southern Baptist minister and wanted one from the Southern Baptist Convention. Dr. Prince is the only Southern Baptist pastor ever to serve a New Zealand church.

Baptist Tabernacle, Auckland, New Zealand

He closed his work at Effingham on Sunday, August 5, 1951, and he and Mrs. Prince left St. Louis on Monday, August 6, bound for New Zealand. It was a breath-taking experience to go so far from home and loved ones, and for the first time Dr. and Mrs. Prince realized what it means for missionaries to go out from home. In fact, they were themselves on a missionary journey. They went from St. Louis to Dallas, Texas for a farewell evening with all his children, and on Tuesday started their long flight by air to New Zealand, via Los Angeles, Honolulu, Canton Island and the Fiji Islands. Because of plane trouble in Honolulu they did not reach Auckland until 10:00 p.m. on Sunday, August 12. They began work with the Tabernacle on Sunday, August 19, 1951. This sojourn in New Zealand was an experience of a lifetime.

The natives of the Pacific Islands are Polynesians, known by various names in the different islands. The name *Maori* is given the natives of New Zealand. The Maori is innately religious and has great power of adaptation. He needs above all the Gospel of Christ. The Polynesians are easy to win to Christ. The islands of the Pacific would be resounding today with the praises of our God if only the Christian people of the world had given them the Gospel. Their failure to do so is a tragedy unspeakable, and perhaps we should say unforgivable.

English people went to New Zealand many years ago and sought to subdue the Maoris and take over their land. Unable to conquer the Maoris by war, they suggested that they all live together in peace. During the Victorian period some great Christian men came from England to New Zealand. The First Baptist Church in New Zealand was constituted in 1851 in the city of Nelson, and four years later the Auckland Baptist Tabernacle came into existence. For more than a century the Baptist Tabernacle has been the leading Baptist church in the Dominion and is sometimes called the Mother Church. This church has brought many great preachers to New Zealand. About one-fourth of the Baptist churches of New Zealand grew out of the Tabernacle and every Baptist church in New Zealand has received financial aid from it. The Tabernacle owns a whole block of property in the adjoining business district and the rental income from these places of business is divided among the churches of New Zealand as they have need each year. In addition, donations are sent to the work on foreign mission fields sponsored by New Zealand Baptists.

Among the great men who came to New Zealand was Rev. Thomas Spurgeon, son of Charles H. Spurgeon, London's great preacher. The biographer of Thomas says that he was not "a chip off the old block, but the old block itself." He was soon called to the pastorate of the Tabernacle. His congregations outgrew their house of worship and he went to England and raised the money to erect the great Tabernacle building. It is a replica of the Spurgeon Metropolitan Tabernacle in London and takes on added significance since the London Tabernacle was destroyed in the second World War. The Baptist Tabernacle building was erected in 1885 and is the largest building of its type on earth south of the equator.

The pulpit Bible used by Charles H. Spurgeon in London was sent to the New Zealand Tabernacle after the London Tabernacle was destroyed in the second World War, and is used in worship services in Auckland each Sunday. The furniture in the pastor's study was used by Thomas Spurgeon many years ago. On the walls of the study are large pictures of thirty-five great ministers who had preached in the Tabernacle pulpit. The great men of the world have stood in that pulpit and preached to throngs of people.

To such a setting Dr. Prince came on August 19, 1951. It was a thrilling experience. The English people are a people of the Book. They are Bible students. They want and demand expository preaching. One-half hour before each preaching service they gather in groups in various rooms of that great Tabernacle building to engage in prayer. The Training Union is held on Saturday night and the Sunday School on Sunday afternoon. The preaching service is preceded only by the prayer meetings in which all participate. Promptly at the hour for worship service the people file into the great auditorium through doors on all sides. There is no talking, not even a whisper. When ushered to their places they sit down and bow their heads in silent prayer. Any preacher can see that this is proper preparation for a great service—and great services they were.

English churches are not so evangelistic as are American

churches. Invitations to profess faith in Christ and unite with a church are seldom given at the close of services as they are in America. Dr. Prince, as was his custom, extended invitations at every service. This practice was barren and unfruitful for the first two months; but one Sunday after a sermon on tithing, eight people came forward on profession of faith. The young man who led the way down the aisle was the son of a missionary, home on furlough. There were tears and sobs throughout the great congregation. The worshippers had never seen a response like that. And what an argument for preaching on giving!

From the time of its organization, more than one hundred years ago, the Auckland Tabernacle had always called men from England to serve as pastors. The present pastor, Rev. F. H. Carter, a native of New Zealand, is the first pastor of the church who has not come from England. From 1949 to 1951, the church had been pastorless because the members had not been able to agree on any man. Perhaps the most helpful service Dr. Prince rendered there was to unite the church and get a pastor called by unanimous vote of the people. It took most of six months to accomplish this task. At length, Rev. John Pritchard of England was called and came to the pastorate there.

The New Zealand Baptist Assembly (Convention) is held annually in November, and sessions continue for ten days. In 1951 this national convention was held in the capital city of Wellington. Each year a featured speaker from abroad is sought for these gatherings. Dr. Prince was the featured speaker for this annual meeting. It was his privilege to preach the convention sermon on Sunday night in the Central Baptist Church. Not only were Baptists from all parts of the Dominion present for this service, but the Mayor of the city, members of the national parliament, and other distinguished guests were present. Dr. Prince read Philippians 2:5-11, and preached on the "Lordship of Christ." This was an inspiring occasion.

Dr. and Mrs. Prince enjoyed to the fullest their stay among the exceedingly gracious and hospitable people of this historic Auckland Tabernacle, and of the lovely country of New Zealand. All too soon their period of service ended and they started homeward on their return journey.

REVIVALS IN HAWAII

Dr. Prince had promised the Southern Baptist Foreign Mission Board that he would hold some revivals in Hawaii on the way home from New Zealand. He and Mrs. Prince left Auckland at 12:00 noon on February 14, 1952, and arrived in Honolulu at 2:00 p.m. on February 14, after a trip of twenty-six hours, the International Date Line entering into the timing. He began a revival on the following Sunday with Pastor J. H. Ware and the people of Nuuanu Church, the second largest Baptist Church in Hawaii. One revival followed another for the next few weeks, and a total of 318 were won to Christ within two months' time. The most fruitful revival held by Dr. Prince during his stay in the Islands was a truly old-fashioned one with Pastor Malcolm Stuart and Olivet Baptist Church, the largest Baptist Church in Hawaii. There were 238 people brought to Christ in this meeting.

The Baptist work in Hawaii was under the direction of the Foreign Mission Board of the Southern Baptist Convention, and missionaries were serving as pastors of the various churches. Several of these missionaries had come to serve in Hawaii after being driven out of other mission fields by the Communists. They were a happy group of workers and it was an inspiration to work with them.

Kinoole Baptist Church

Kinoole Baptist Church is located in Hilo on the Island of Hawaii. Dr. H. B. Ramsour was the pastor of this growing congregation and a new and commodious building had just been finished. On Sunday, March 23, 1952, Dr. Prince brought the message at the dedicatory service. Dr. Ramsour and his family left that week for their furlough in the mainland and Dr. Prince remained to serve as supply pastor. Dr. Ramsour is a graduate of Howard Payne College, Brownwood, Texas, and was a student there while Dr. Prince was pastor of Brownwood First Baptist Church. The Princes enjoyed their period of service in Kinoole Baptist Church.

Hawaiian Baptist Academy

Dr. and Mrs. Prince returned to Honolulu after two months of service with the lovely people of Kinoole Baptist Church, to take up his duties as principal pro tempore of the Hawaiian Baptist Academy. This school—all grades from kindergarten to twelfth grade—had been established seven years before and its founder and faithful principal, Rev. H. P. McCormick, (Mrs. McCormick, a graduate nurse, was the school nurse) had not had a furlough in all that time because there was no one available with suitable experience to direct the school in his absence. Dr. Prince's sojourn in the Islands seemed opportune, and he was asked to take over Principal McCormick's duties for a year. Mrs. Prince taught in the Academy during that year and the following year, and this was a pleasant time of gracious friendships and delightful new experiences.

The Academy opened in September, 1952, with the largest enrollment in its history up to that time. During the school year, a gracious revival was held and sixty students were led to Christ. Dr. James G. Harris, at that time pastor of Beech

Street Baptist Church, Texarkana, Arkansas, was the evangelist. Dr. Harris is one of Dr. Prince's spiritual sons, and was ordained by the First Church, Pineville, Louisiana, while Dr. Prince was pastor there. James is a brother of Miss Josephine Harris, B.S.U. Director at the University of Hawaii.

The year at the Academy was a very happy one and passed all too rapidly. During the year a large concrete building was erected and equipped, and the first four grades were housed in it. The gifts of Southern Baptists through the Lottie Moon Offering made possible this much needed building. Principal and Mrs. McCormick returned in June, 1953. Mrs. Prince continued to teach in the Academy for the next year. Dr. Prince took up his work as President of Honolulu Christian College.

The Baptist Academy now has a much larger faculty and student body and is the best private school in the Islands. A second story has been added to this concrete building which was erected in 1952, and additional property has been purchased adjoining the campus. The Baptist churches in the Islands maintain kindergartens, and one is maintained at the Academy. The one great need of our Baptist work in Hawaii was a good Baptist College.

Waianae Baptist Church

Soon after the Academy opened in September, Dr. Prince was called to preach at the Waianae Mission, some 35 miles from Honolulu. There were about a dozen people at the Mission at that time. He preached for these people about two years and organized Waianae Baptist Church on Sunday, February 22, 1953. This is now one of the great churches of the Baptist work in Hawaii.

This Waianae Mission was at the Baptist Assembly grounds at Puu-Kahea. This is the Ridgecrest of Hawaii. The Waianae

Church has since erected a lovely building adjoining the encampment grounds. This Church has also started four missions in that area of Oahu Island, three of which are now churches and one is yet a mission, started only recently. Four hundred more people are in Sunday School because these missions were started. The Waianae Church now has under construction an educational building adjoining their church. Surely this church is in front rank among Hawaiian Baptist churches and is ministering in a great manner to the Leeward Coastal area. All this has been accomplished since the Waianae Mission was started. Three other pastors have served since Dr. Prince was pastor—Dr. Victor Koon, Rev. Roy Davis, and the present pastor, Rev. Charles D. Mullins. Much credit for the success of the work in Waianae is due to the missionary vision and faithful service of Mr. and Mrs. R. E. Peterson. Mr. Peterson is caretaker of the Assembly grounds. Dr. and Mrs. Prince are justly proud of the work in Waianae. They traveled thousands of miles back and forth to start this work and develop it into a church. Additions were frequent and baptisms a common occurrence in the program. Waianae is a lovely little city with many happy people in and around the city. The church is making its influence felt in all that strategic area. The coming of Baptists from all the Islands to various encampment programs is a great encouragement to the faithful workers at Waianae.

Honolulu Christian College

Mention has already been made of Dr. Prince's venture into the presidency at Ewing College and Hannibal-LaGrange College, and of his term as principal of the Hawaiian Baptist Academy in Honolulu. This would seem to be enough, but another task was in store for him.

When he went to Hawaii there were two institutions of higher education—the University of Hawaii, and Jackson

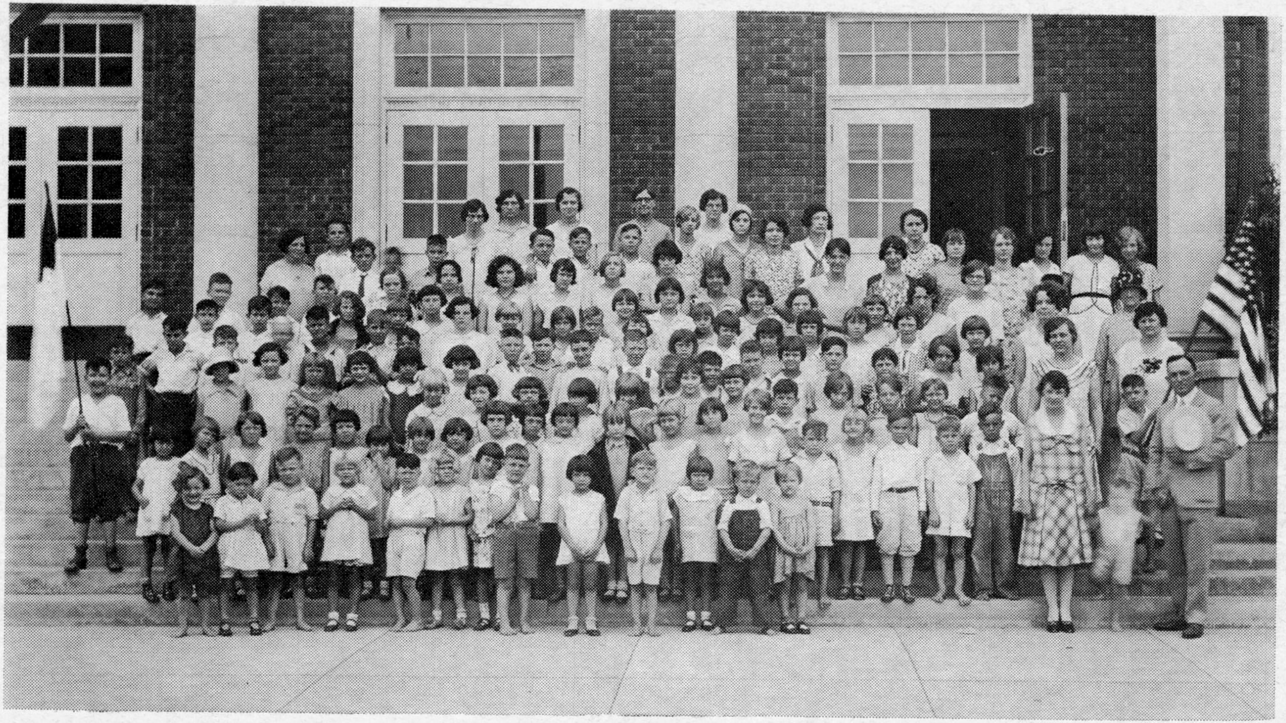

First Vacation Bible school conducted by Miss Beulah Doerr in Brownwood, Texas, in 1928 "way back when" Bible schools were something new in our church.

President Prince and Board of Trustees, Honolulu Christian College, Honolulu, Hawaii — 1953.

College, a small struggling institution in Honolulu. Dr. Lew Barrett was president of Jackson College and pastor of the First Baptist Church. The school did not have the cooperation of the various churches and was not accredited. There was a feeling that there should be a good College that was able to secure the cooperation of the churches and offer accredited work. No denomination was financially able to start a college at that time. A movement was started to found a Christian College that all could support. After many preliminary meetings and much prayer and consideration of the problem, a charter was secured and Honolulu Christian College was founded. Dr. Prince was present in the preliminary meetings and served as advisor in the work of starting the College. He was the only man in Honolulu who had previous experience as a College President. The Board sought for a President from the mainland but none could be secured. Finally, on April 21, 1953, he was elected as the first president of the College. It was exactly twelve years before—April 21, 1941—that he was elected President of Hannibal-LaGrange College.

The College Board was composed of people from the various evangelical churches, and the school was Christian but non-denominational. This was all they could do. His task was to secure a location for the school, find a faculty and students. This required a whole summer. A goodly number of the members of the Board of Trustees were Baptists—not by design, but by the fact that these would serve. The majority of the faculty members were also Baptists. Dr. Thomas J. Talbert of Missouri University was secured as Dean, and the College opened the first of September with a small but very choice group of students. The College was planned to meet all requirements for accreditation and all teachers were qualified to offer accredited work.

Owing to the distance from Waianae, Dr. Prince asked to be released from his pastorate there, and he became supply pastor for Olivet Baptist Church, the largest Baptist Church

President Prince in his office at Honolulu Christian College.

in Hawaii. Pastor Malcolm Stuart was in the mainland on furlough for four months. There were additions at about every service, and baptisms were frequent. He had the privilege of leading a number of people of various nationalities to Christ, and baptizing them. After the return of Pastor Stuart he was called as pastor of the First Baptist Church, and held this position until he left Honolulu. All the while he was living in the President's home on the campus and directing the work of the College. The Board and faculty and cooperating churches were universally gracious and prayerfully helpful in the work, and the little College moved along in a very fine manner. Excellent work was done in the class rooms and good grades were made by the students of various nationalities who were enrolled.

The great need was money, for all cooperating in this movement were poor people. The National Association of Evangelicals was cooperating in the mainland and gave some financial help. When Dean Talbert decided to return to the mainland, Dr. L. Paul Gresham was secured as Dean and he did much to give direction to the curricula and activities of the school. He was an educator of the first order, with a Ph.D. from Vanderbilt University.

Honolulu Christian College was founded to meet a great need. Five thousand of the young people who were graduating from High School each year had no chance to secure higher education because the University of Hawaii was crowded to capacity. After Dr. Prince came to the mainland Dr. Gresham was elected President and served in a very effective manner. When Dr. Gresham returned to the mainland Rev. Robert Loveless was elected President. The lack of money and equipment has prevented this College from accomplishing what its founders dreamed of accomplishing. The need was great, the College well founded scholastically and doing accredited work, but was forever handicapped by lack of funds. This college has just merged with Hawaii Pacific College (1966) and good reports come of the progress of the work.

Mention has already been made of the return of Dr. Prince to the mainland to celebrate his fiftieth anniversary in the ministry at Barnhill Baptist Church. He came also to search for money for the College. He traveled much and over widely spread areas in the search of money but found very little help. It was a very discouraging task. The churches of the National Association of Evangelicals were gracious and received him cordially, but all of them were already committed to help other projects in Honolulu as well as in the mainland. It was his intention to return to Honolulu and the College when he came away, but after more than a year of unsuccessful effort to raise money he resigned as President and Dr. Gresham was elected to succeed him.

Since Honolulu Christian College was founded the Catholics, the Seventh Day Adventists and the Mormons have built great colleges in Honolulu and nearby. The field was wide open when Honolulu Christian College was started. The evangelical churches of Honolulu and the mainland missed their opportunity to capture many of Honolulu's fine young people to educate them in a Christian school.

At any rate, he had a most delightful time as President of this young college. It was with deepest regret that he gave up his work. The Board of Regents were thoroughly cooperative at all times and the best of harmony prevailed. Dr. Prince wishes he could live those days over again. He can never forget the great crowds of young people who needed an education and to whom he tried to minister. This was his third and last attempt as a college president.

VIII.

THE RETURN TO THE HOMELAND

A thousand precious memories bound Dr. and Mrs. Prince to New Zealand and Hawaii as they started toward the homeland. Their "missionary journey" had been a blessed experience and many had been won to Christ.

Fiftieth Anniversary

Through the years of his ministry, Dr. Prince had held before him the dream of returning to his old home church, where he was ordained, to preach on his fiftieth anniversary. He and Mrs. Prince flew in from Hawaii in 1954 for this celebration. The anniversary date was Saturday, May 29, 1954. The celebration was held at Barnhill Baptist Church, Barnhill, Illinois, on Sunday, May 30, 1954, at 2:30 p.m. The day dawned clear and beautiful—a lovely spring day.

The "Boy Preacher" of 1904 was now 50 years older. Barnhill Baptist Church was crowded for the service but only three persons were present who heard his first sermon 50 years ago. (These have since gone on to be with the Lord). But many others were there whom he had known through most of his work in Southern Illinois, and it was a wonderful day of renewing friendships and meeting children and grandchildren of friends of the earlier years. Dr. Prince preached the anniversary sermon on the subject: "The Message We Preach."

At this service, Dr. Prince was presented a Memory Book containing greetings from many with whom he had worked during the years. This writer has looked over many of the letters and selected a few to present to our readers.

Dr. John L. Hill
Book Editor
Baptist Sunday School Board

I am happy to join your large company of friends in extending felicitations on this significant anniversary. Yours has been and still is a life of busy service for our Lord, and in every relationship you have manifested the spirit of efficient selflessness which has won the appreciation of all associated with you.

Our contacts, all too infrequent for me, have always been pleasant and inspiring, and I am happy in the privilege of calling you friend. I rejoice in your continued usefulness.

Dan S. C. Liu
Chief of Police, Honolulu
President, International Police Association

Mrs. Liu and I extend heartiest congratulations upon the Fiftieth Anniversary of your ordination. We are greatly impressed by your many, many years of commendable service for the Lord. It has been my great privilege to have worked with you closely during the past year, and because of that association my life has been made that much richer. May God continue to bless you as you carry on in His ministry.

Dr. T. L. Holcomb
Executive Secretary
Baptist Sunday School Board

I rejoice in the favor of God upon your ministry for a half century. It is remarkable that you have been permitted to preach His glorious gospel in so many parts of the world. I appreciate your personal friendship. I have counted it an honor and privilege to know you for many years. May the remaining years of your ministry be the richest of your long and successful career.

Dr. John W. Raley, President
Oklahoma Baptist University
Shawnee, Oklahoma

Let me join your many friends in congratulating you on the fiftieth anniversary of service in the ministry. Certainly the variety of service as well as the tenure has brought to you a wealth in expression and in growth that cannot be measured. May God bless you and lead you as you approach climax days.

Dr. J. C. Wells
Baptist City Missionary
New Orleans, Louisiana

Allow me to congratulate you on your Fiftieth Anniversary as a minister. I knew you had been an active man, doing a lot of things in a lot of places, but really I did not know you had gone so far and done so much and worked so long as you have. I know of no one who has a record equal to your record. You have set an example for our young ministers. You have been an inspiration to me and I shall always treasure the moments that we have had together.

Dr. John W. Bradbury, Editor
The Watchman-Examiner
New York, New York

Let me join the great company that will send you congratulations on your Fiftieth Anniversary as a Christian Minister. It is remarkable how much you have crowded into your useful life. The Watchman-Examiner family will rejoice with you over the attainment of your 50-year record. We pray that God's blessings will rest upon all who have received the Word of God through you and upon all who have been built up in the most holy faith. What a great company they make!

You must belong to the Lord's reserves. When there is an emergency, He calls upon you and you are there and able. I thought you were in the Hawaiian Islands and here I learn that you are in Florida. It is difficult keeping track of you. Your maturity means a great deal to our Baptist cause.

Dr. A. S. Newman
State Brotherhood Secretary
Louisiana

Congratulations on your Fiftieth Anniversary. Yours has been a long, useful, fruitful and varied ministry.

While checking over your fields of service I do not observe mention of your leadership in the 1937 campaign to save Louisiana College. While the over-all goal was not reached—as you will remember—the financial pressure was relieved and the school was saved. You and your co-workers were used of the Lord to save this great institution. I know you will rejoice to know that the College is now secure, and is giving a great service to our Lord and the Baptist cause around the world. Greetings, congratulations, and best wishes for many more fruitful years of service.

Dr. George J. Mason
Secretary-Emeritus
Baptist Foundation of Texas

Friend, you have made a wonderful record for the Lord during these fifty years. You have been a very versatile servant and you have made good in many capacities during this time. With it all, however, you have majored in evangelism and the Lord has blessed you greatly. Your friendship has meant a lot to me during all these years, and may the Lord be near and precious to you to the end of the days.

Dr. John W. Dowdy, President
Southwest Baptist College

I want to join your many friends in expressing to you my greetings and best wishes on the occasion of the celebration of your Fiftieth Anniversary as an ordained minister. I hope that May 30th will be one of the greatest days you have experienced up to this time.

Rev. William E. Young
Director of Activities
Calder Baptist Church
Texas

Congratulations on this, the Fiftieth Anniversary of your ordination to the Gospel ministry. How long is fifty years? According to the calendar, it can be easily figured; according to the results, one must deal in eternal values—and that means endless measurement.

Those whom you have baptized, welcomed into the Baptist Churches—influenced in one Academy and three Colleges, and won to Christ and into the churches through evangelistic ministries—all rise up and call you blessed.

A great host like Juel and me have entered through the doors of personal friendship and labors together in Christian service. We have felt the beat of your heart, the burden of your soul and the direction of your life. We, too, stand up and are counted among those whom you have touched and helped. Your sharing and caring have been a source of genuine helpfulness. Blessings on you.

STEWARDSHIP EVANGELIST

At some time in the late 1940's, Dr. B. C. Land, one of the most capable of stewardship evangelists among Southern Baptists, had turned from the pastorate to give himself wholly to the work of stewardship evangelism. He founded the Stewardship Evangelism Association at Jackson, Mississippi and had enlisted a number of men in strategic places as helpers in his work. When Dr. Prince returned from his work overseas, he was invited to be listed among Dr. Land's workers. After resigning from Honolulu Christian College, he became Dr. Land's first assistant and began work in this field. He was in California in a series of four such consecutive stewardship revivals when he received a telegram from Mrs. Land stating that Dr. Land had suddenly passed to his heavenly home, and asking him to return to Jackson at his earliest convenience to take over his work. Dr. Land had a wonderful work started. He had written a number of books on stewardship and had an excellent supply of posters and other literature for use in promotion. Nothing has been prepared elsewhere which equals the material prepared by this capable and perceptive man. He had traveled to many states holding one-week stewardship revivals with outstanding results.

Mrs. Land directed the Stewardship Publishing Company and the dispatching of literature to all the widespread areas from which requests came. She graciously welcomed Dr. Prince, and he went to work in earnest as Stewardship Director of the organization. He and Mrs. Prince traveled from Florida to California and back and forth from coast to coast in Stewardship revivals. These were some of the happy days of his ministry. He met with good success in setting up church budgets and directing financial campaigns in the churches. It was a work that needed to be done, and he had a plan that was informational, inspirational and notably successful.

He would have gladly continued in this work until this day but for one thing that got in the way. Southern Baptist "Forward Program of Church Finance" was started the following year. He felt that if he continued in his work he would appear to be working in opposition to the program of the denomination to which he has always been loyal. He therefore gave up this work when the "Forward Program of Church Finance" was announced for Southern Baptists. His venture in this field was a blessing to him and a help to the churches.

FIRST CHURCH, LAFAYETTE, LOUISIANA

Mention has already been made of the fact that Dr. Prince served as pastor of two of Louisiana's strong churches—Pineville and West Monroe. On June 1, 1957, he went to Lafayette First Church as interim pastor. On August 14th he was unanimously called to serve as pastor for at least a year to give the Pulpit Committee time to find a pastor. It has been pointed out earlier in this manuscript that only one of his interim pastorates has ever closed on time.

The First Church, Lafayette, is one of Louisiana's leading churches. The edge of the campus of Southwestern Louisiana University is only three blocks away and many of the faculty members and students hold membership in this church. Many faithful workers are found in this church and they have a mind to work. Dr. Prince served fifteen months as pastor of this lovely people. It was agreed that Mrs. Prince should be relieved of responsibility to the church that she might complete her graduate work and receive her Master's degree.

Large crowds attended the church services and there were additions at practically every service—a total of 218 additions, with 70 of them by baptism. The budget was increased and easily subscribed. The sojourn with this church was most pleasant. The people loved their pastor and followed his leadership faithfully. It was difficult to turn from such a happy situation, but on September 1, 1958, he closed his work there and moved to St. Louis. Mrs. Prince had accepted a position as teacher in Jennings Elementary School—a position she has held since that time. The good people of Lafayette gave them a farewell party and a liberal gift of money and advised their retiring pastor to rest a while before taking other work. He certainly needed the rest, and he will ever be grateful to those good people, who by their generosity enabled him to have a short period of reduced activity before beginning full time work in a new assignment.

IMMANUEL BAPTIST MISSION

Dr. Prince's next assignment was a very pleasant task. Unity-Roselawn Baptist Church was sponsoring a mission at Scott Field Air Force Base. He was asked by the Church to preach for this mission. He began work there in December, 1958, and served exactly one year.

A very fine group of Baptist men were among the servicemen stationed at Scott Field at that time and they came from all parts of the United States. They were the "cream of the crop" from the various churches from which they had come. It was a joy to work with them. They were ready and willing to undertake any task their pastor suggested. The building in which they worshipped was erected by Unity-Roselawn but was not finished inside. Only the ground floor was usable. The men set to work to complete the second floor and made of it a beautiful auditorium. A good program was carried on—Sunday School, Training Union, W.M.S., Vacation Bible School and other activities. There were no problems. All were united. All were happy. All were at work. The membership shifted because of the transfer of men in military service, but others came in their places. There was only one resident family not involved in military service and that was Don Gilmore and his family. Don was a deacon of Unity-Roselawn Church and went out to help establish the mission. He is a good Bible student and a valuable church worker. He was an inspiration to his pastor at all times. In the late summer of 1959, a large contingent of Baptist men were among those transferred out and this was a hard blow to the mission. It was exceedingly difficult for Dr. and Mrs. Prince to leave these dear people, but they closed their work at the end of December.

Dr. and Mrs. Prince still receive letters from people once in Immanuel, and now in many parts of the world. The Immanuel Mission is now a Baptist Church and still ministering to the families in service at Scott Field Air Force Base.

IX.

A CLOSE-UP VIEW

Some one has said that a man can be measured by the height of his vision, the width of his sympathies, the depth of his convictions, and the length of his endurance. He can also be measured by the reaction of others to him, whether favorable or unfavorable. Paul had a revival or a riot everywhere he went, and whichever it turned out to be was determined by the reaction of the people.

The Man as Others See Him

This author feels that the reader ought to know of the statements of others who were contemporaries of Dr. Prince. He has hundreds of letters of commendation from men who worked with him in the former days. He has copies of resolutions adopted by the churches he has served—almost everyone of them—and from Associations and State Boards where he served in the yester-years. It was the privilege of this writer to see these documents and to gather a few from the many he has received.

DR. GEORGE W. TRUETT, PASTOR
First Baptist Church
Dallas, Texas

On the occasion of Dr. Prince's removal from Dallas to the pastorate at First Church, Pineville, Louisiana, Dr. Truett wrote in 1934:

"On my recent return home from the trip overseas, I have learned, with great pleasure, that you have again taken up the duties of the pastorate. We shall miss you from our dear church here, where you and your family are held in such high esteem by us all, and we shall miss you from Texas as well. But happily you are not far away from us in your present location, and we shall hope to see you again and again, face to face. You may be fully assured that you shall be given a large and abiding place in our hearts and prayers. And these greetings likewise include your dear wife and children. May heaven's best blessing attend you, all and each, both for today and for the long tomorrow!"

The last time Dr. Truett and Dr. Prince met was in the State-wide conference in Sedalia, Missouri, in March, 1942. Following this three-day session, Dr. Truett wrote on April 8, 1942:

"You have indeed made me your deeply grateful debtor by the gracious letter that you have written me concerning my visit, a little while ago, to Sedalia. Your words cheered me more than I can say, and from my deepest heart I thank you for them. Let me also rejoice with you, with all my heart, in your great achievement with your college. Your achievement is notable, and many of us on the outside must join you and yours in devoutest thanksgiving to God for His great favor upon you there. My best wishes for you and all your household, and for your immeasurably important work, both for today and for all the unfolding future!"

DR. J. B. LAWRENCE
Executive Secretary
Home Mission Board

Thank you for your letter and the information it brings, that Hannibal-LaGrange College is out of debt. This is a glorious achievement, and places the College in a position where it can render great service in the advancement of the Kingdom. I congratulate you on the splendid service which you have rendered in bringing this institution out of debt. Blessings on you, my Brother, in the great work you are doing!

DR. P. S. LANYON
Executive Secretary
Baptist Union of New Zealand

I would like to write a word of appreciation of your ministry at the Baptist Tabernacle, Auckland. You came at a very difficult time in the history of this church and served faithfully and well. Our people there were benefitted by your ministry, and we pray that wherever you may go you may continue the remarkable work you have been doing through the years.

DR. L. E. MARTIN, PASTOR
Second Baptist Church
Hopkinsville, Kentucky

The life and work of Dr. A. E. Prince as pastor, evangelist, educator, and denominational worker, have been a source of inspiration to me through the years. My appreciation of Dr. Prince as a faithful and fruitful servant of the Lord deepens as his work continues under the blessing of God.

As pastor of the Second Baptist Church, Hopkinsville, Kentucky, I was fortunate to secure him as evangelist of one of our revivals. The meeting resulted in 91 additions to the church, the largest harvest we have ever reaped in a single meeting. Dr. Prince was universally loved and respected by our people. The influence of his work continued to bless our people long after he was gone.

DR. C. E. AUTREY
Superintendent of Evangelism
Southern Baptist Convention

Dr. A. E. Prince was one of the finest, most wholesome pastor-evangelists the State of Louisiana has ever had. Dr. Prince was instrumental in revolutionizing the organization and finances of the First Baptist Church of West Monroe, Louisiana. And while doing this very necessary piece of pastoral work, he opened the gates to a limitless field of evangelism in that community. The First Church, West Monroe, continues to build on the foundations laid by this far-sighted and consecrated pastor.

JAMES M. WORK, ASSOCIATE-PASTOR
Gordon Street Baptist Church
Atlanta, Georgia

I take pleasure in stating that Dr. A. E. Prince was the evangelist in one of the best revivals that Gordon Street

Baptist Church has ever had. Dr. Prince came to us on the invitation of the late Dr. T. F. Harvey, at that time pastor of the church. Our people were greatly revived and stirred to action by the wonderful messages of this great preacher. There were about 100 additions to the church during the revival. I had the happy privilege of directing the music for this revival.

REV. HARLEY HENDERSON, PASTOR
First Baptist Church
Broken Bow, Nebraska

Dr. and Mrs. Prince won their way in the hearts of our people during the very first service of the revival and became increasingly adored as the days went by. The winsome smile of Mrs. Prince gave her a personal magnetism that added to the beauty of her spirit and the tender persuasive quality so evident in her singing. Surely the love of Christ was exemplified in the lives of these two people.

OUR NEIGHBOR MOVED*

We have just told Dr. A. E. Prince and his family, goodbye. They are now on their way to Pineville, Louisiana, where he goes to be pastor of the First Baptist Church. Pineville is where the Baptists of Louisiana have located their college. It seems that Dr. Prince is predestinated and foreordained to be pastor in a Baptist College town, as he has had such a field all of his ministerial life.

Dr. Prince is a good preacher. He has supplied acceptably at the First Baptist Church of Dallas more than once. He has been the most incessantly busy denominational man we ever knew. How he has kept going day and night has been a marvel to us who have lived next door. We wish for him, Mrs. Prince, their three daughters and "Junior" all happiness and success and every good that can bless their lives. We shall be happy to see any of them back in Dallas any time.

* Dr. Prince and family lived next door to Dr. and Mrs. F. M. McConnell while they sojourned in Dallas. Dr. McConnell was editor of the Texas Baptist Standard and this article appeared in the Standard the week the Prince family moved to Pineville.

AUTHOR

Dr. Prince has written a number of books, and three were written while he served as president at Hannibal. He compiled two books of sermons by Louisiana ministers—Life's Best, and Meeting Life's Reverses. He has printed two books of his own sermons—Christ is All, and Back to Bethel. He has written two histories—History of Fifth Street Baptist Church, and History of Ewing College. He has printed a book of twenty of his Christmas messages, sent out, one each year, from 1924-1944. He has had many letters of appreciation and reviews of his books. We have selected some for publication in this volume.

DR. E. GODBOLD
General Superintendent
Missouri Baptist General Convention
November 27, 1940

I read your book last night, the first evening I have had at home for a long time, and I appreciate it very highly. You have made a contribution in this volume to sermonology. We need more of the sort of sermons carried in this volume (Christ is All), that is, sermons that are evangelistic and yet not frothy, that contain a well rounded Gospel message. Let me thank you for your substantial contribution. Frankly, I am not very strong on reading sermons but when I got started on yours I could not stop until I had finished it. It is very seldom that I read one sermon through.

DR. J. R. GRANT, PRESIDENT
Ouachita College
Arkadelphia, Arkansas
December 20, 1940

Three books, "Christ is All," "Meeting Life's Reverses," and "Life's Best" have helped us spend a better Christmas vacation. The Ouachita College students join in expressing appreciation for the two copies of "Christ is All" and "Meeting Life's Reverses." The Librarian feels sure we shall have to order extra copies to meet the demand of the students.

REVIEW OF BACK TO BETHEL
Dr. John L. Hill
Book Editor
Baptist Sunday School Board
November 15, 1942

These soulful sermons from the heart of the scholarly pastor-College President go direct to the heart of the reader. If one is looking for the speculative, the theoretical, the imaginary, the abstract, he may pass this volume by; but they who hunger for spiritual food, presented in most appetizing form, will linger over these satisfying messages. There are twelve sermons in this collection, nine of them based on Old Testament texts, and the others use two texts, one of which is from the Old Testament. For the most part this is a volume for young people; certain sermons, however, have peculiar application. Every preacher should read "A Lesson for Preachers;" every mature person will enjoy and profit by "Back to Bethel" and "The Old Fashioned Christian Home." Each serman is enriched by gems from literature and from experience, and breathes the compassionate, radiant spirit of the consecrated Author; this is a good book and cannot be read without helpfulness to the reader.

DR. NOEL M. TAYLOR, VICE PRESIDENT
Broadway Plan, Inc.
Houston, Texas

Quite some time ago you gave me three of your books—"History of Ewing College," "Life's Best," and "Back to Bethel." I took these along for reading on a trip this week to several of the far western states. The purpose of this note is to thank you again for the books and for the blessing I received from reading them. Especially do I want to thank you for the messages in the book, "Back to Bethel." Most sermon books fall tremendously short of what we could hope. This one, however, is an exception. Your book is a vital message presented in a clear and readable manner. It is one of the best books of sermons to come to my attention.

DR. B. C. LAND, PASTOR
First Baptist Church
Quincy, Florida

"Christ is All" is the title of a volume of twelve challenging, dynamic, Christ-centered, Christ-exalting, Gospel messages by Dr. A. E. Prince, President of the Executive Board of the Louisiana Baptist Convention and the successful pastor of the First Baptist Church, West Monroe, Louisiana. The author is one of the most popular and successful pastor-evangelists in "Lovely Louisiana." In addition to his heavy and exacting duties as President of the Executive Board and pastor of a great church of 2,000 or more members, he conducts a number of evangelistic meetings each year, and always with good success. Practical in application, vigorous in style, apt in illumination, rich in Scripture quotations, compassionate in appeal, refreshing in treatment, and evangelistic in content, these sermons will prove a distinct blessing to every one who has the good fortune to read them.

DR. JULIAN ATWOOD, PASTOR
First Baptist Church
Texarkana, Texas

I have known the author of this book (Christ is All) for many years, and have heard him deliver many great sermons, and I believe for clearness of expression, forcefulness of thought, and dignity of style, none exceeds this collection, the title of which is taken from the subject of the first sermon.

As a lifelong friend of the author, it is a peculiar joy to have in permanent form this volume so rich in Biblical truth, so filled with spiritual power, and of beautiful diction. Dr. Prince has succeeded well in translating some of these sermons into the printed page so that the reader gets much of the inspiration of the speaker's oral messages. I heartily recommend this book as a valuable addition to any library.

MAKING DECISIONS

In his great sermon on the subject: "Every Man's Life a Plan of God," Horace Bushnell said: "God has a definite life-plan for every human being, guarding him visibly or invisibly for some exact purpose which it would be the true significance and glory of his life to have accomplished." To this statement we all can agree. One of life's greatest discoveries is to find that life-plan.

Dr. Prince holds that many do not start at the right place in their efforts to make decisions. There is a decision which takes precedence over all other decisions and opens the way to the proper choices in all other matters, and that decision is who shall be the Lord of our lives. There are two possible centers of life—Christ or self. Dr. S. D. Gordon said: "In the heart of every saved person is a cross and a throne. The cross is for self and the throne is for Christ, and we shall have power in proportion as self in on the cross and Christ is on the throne."

When our lives are given in a sustained dedication to Christ, and Jesus is crowned Lord over all for us, one has but to listen for a voice behind him saying: "This is the way; walk ye in it." In one of the supremely decisive moments in the life of Robert Louis Stevenson, he gave this personal testimony: "I came about like a well-handled ship. There stood at the wheel that Unknown Oarsman whom we call God."

Our choices make us what we are, and we are never the same again after we make a choice. This is true in every relationship of life. Our destiny hinges on our choices. We walk by faith, not by sight, and therefore, the path is sometimes not too clearly discerned because of our lack of faith. There is much human weakness about us.

Dr. Prince claims no magic power to make decisions. He admits that all of us flounder about in our stupidity. He has always sought to find out how great men live, and serve, and make their decisions, and he carefully applies what he learns from them in reaching decisions in the affairs of his own life. Early in his ministry he found the simple guide lines used by

George Mueller in seeking to find the will of God, and he has followed these throughout his ministry. George Mueller points the way in these lines:

> 1. I seek at the beginning to get my heart into such a state that it has no will of its own in regard to a given matter. Nine-tenths of the trouble with people is just here. Nine-tenths of the difficulties are overcome when our hearts are willing and ready to do God's will, whatever it may be. When one is in this state, it is usually but a little way to the knowledge of what His will is.
>
> 2. Having done this, I do not leave the result to feeling or simple impression. If I do so, I make myself liable to get delusions.
>
> 3. I seek the will of the Spirit of God through or in connection with, the Word of God. The Spirit and the Word must be combined. If I look to the Spirit alone without the Word, I lay myself open to great delusions also. If the Holy Spirit guides us at all, He will do it according to the Scriptures and never contrary to them.
>
> 4. Next, I take into account providential circumstances. These often plainly indicate God's will in connection with His Word and Spirit.
>
> 5. I ask God in prayer to reveal His will to me aright.
>
> 6. Thus through prayer to God, the study of His Word, and reflection, I come to a deliberate judgment according to the best of my ability and knowledge, and if my mind is thus at peace, and continues so after two or three more petitions, I proceed accordingly.
>
> In trivial matters, and in transactions involving most important issues, I have found this method effective.

Dr. Prince insists that the highest level of Christian living and service is reached only—

> 1. When the heart is right with God.
>
> 2. When unfaltering obedience and unwavering loyalty to God has joined the assurance of Divine favor upon one's life.
>
> 3. When we can say at all times, and under all circumstances, "Thy will be done."
>
> 4. When the chief desire of one's life is that God should work in him "to will and to do of His own good pleasure."

Dr. Prince emphasizes always the fact that much use must be made of prayer and of the Word of God and always under the direction of the Holy Spirit. There are no short cuts to the goal in this matter. A pillar of cloud and fire led the Israelites in the long ago, and the same God leads His people today. One must constantly watch for tokens of His leadership. God still moves in the tops of the mulberry trees and often speaks with a still small voice to those who are listening.

PREPARING SERMONS

Dr. Prince says that one difference between him and Charles Haddon Spurgeon is that Spurgeon parted his hair on the right side and Dr. Prince parts his on the left. He adds with a smile that there are other areas in which he and the great London preacher differ, the greatest being in preaching ability.

Charles H. Spurgeon spent his time during the week in reading. On Saturday night after supper he went into his study and prepared the outline for his sermon for the following day. For this, he drew on his store of knowledge gained in his reading during the week. Of course, he had the preparation of prayer and a keen understanding of the needs of the people to whom he ministered. Above all, he was a man of destiny—called of God and dedicated to the work of the ministry—and he walked with God. He was a humble man who knew the Lord and preferred His will above all else.

Henry Ward Beecher used a different method. He described his practice in these words:

> "I have a dozen or more topics lying loose in my mind through the week; I think of one or another as occasion may serve, anywhere, at home, in the street, in the horse-car. I rarely know what theme I shall use until Sunday morning. Then, after breakfast I go into my study as a man goes into his orchard; I feel among these themes as he feels among his apples, to find the ripest and best. The theme which seems most ripe I pluck; then I select my text, analyze my subject, prepare the outline and go into the pulpit to preach it while it is fresh."

Like other preachers, Henry Ward Beecher admitted that sometimes on Sunday he could not use the material he had found through the week. Some new theme would grip his heart and he had to preach it.

Dr. Prince follows both of these plans. He tries to have his sermon subjects for the following Sunday in mind early in the week; and, as opportunity affords, all through the week he reads material germane to the subjects. He sets aside Saturday for sermon preparation and tries to avoid interruptions of his work hours on that day. But sometimes he gropes all week trying to find subjects for Sunday. In such cases he spends Saturday in his study alone with God, seeking God's message. If his "wheels spin" over the Spurgeon method on Saturday, he tries the Beecher method before each service on Sunday.

He uses various methods of preaching—textual, topical and expository. His first choice is expository, but much of his preaching is textual and topical. When he has decided on a certain Scripture, he reads what is found in the several sets of commentaries, and also reads other men's sermons which have been preached on this Scripture. Many of his illustrations are from his own experience.

Although he admits having resorted to it on occasion, he does not recommend what he calls "shotgun preaching." In the early days, most preachers had few books and not much other reading material. They put together what they found—related or not—and when the time came to preach, shot the whole load at the congregation. Likewise, old-time doctors are said to have kept a large bottle in their offices. When they found a drug they did not know what to do with, they put it in the bottle and as time passed added to these other drugs they did not know. When they had a patient whose affliction they did not know, they gave the patient a dose of this mixture.

It usually cured or killed. This is probably the outcome of "shotgun preaching."

Dr. Prince sometimes feels led to change the text and the message even while the special music is being rendered before the sermon. When he rises to preach at such times, he casts aside all his previous plans and presents the text which has so suddenly taken hold of him. Then for the next half hour he tries to keep self out of the way so that the Lord can deliver his particular message for that hour to both the people and the preacher. Those who hear him oftenest regard this as his best preaching. They say that when he reads a text over about twice, lays down his Bible, takes a good look at his congregation and "takes off," they know that things are going to happen. He says jokingly that he likes this method of preaching because there is no time in advance to worry over this sermon. But actually there is something exhilarating and solemnizing about being used in this overwhelmingly direct way as God's mouthpiece, and this something adds conviction to the voice and manner of the preacher as he speaks, and lingers with him for hours afterward.

It is Dr. Prince's abiding conviction that the matter of sermon preparation reaches far back of any labor in one's study on Saturday. He holds that the first part of the preparation of every sermon a man will ever preach is completed when he responds to the divine call to preach. The second part develops in the very act of standing still and waiting, for just as Paul went into Arabia for the space of three years to get his message, so must the preacher tarry long alone with God if he wants a message. No one can enter into this experience with him. God's message must become so much a part of the preacher that the preacher's soul is set on fire with the message. A God-called man is a God-intoxicated soul. Preaching is divine energy operating through human personality for divine purposes. God's preacher must be a Spirit-led man. Perhaps few men among us have preached as much about the Holy Spirit as has Dr. Prince. He seeks ever to be a Spirit-filled man.

The third part in the preparation of a sermon is a continuum, residing in the preacher's daily effort to follow the Lord. E. M. Bounds said:

> It is not great talents or great learning or great preachers that God needs, but men great in holiness, great in faith, great in love, great in fidelity, great for God—men always preaching by holy sermons in the pulpit, by holy lives out of it. These can mould a generation for God.

Every true preacher is an ambassador for Christ. He is a herald bearing good tidings. Our English word for preacher does not support the dignity or the challenge of the original word, which signifies a proclamation made to a crowd of people in a public square. In early days the appearance of the herald in the market place was the occasion for the eager assembling of the populace, because the herald carried imperial tidings. Paul thought of himself as a herald in this sense. And this should be the thinking of every preacher.

God's message is entrusted to God-called men. God calls his messengers and gives them the message he wants them to preach. How immeasurably important it is that the preacher tarry with God until he finds God's message for the people. Then he will preach that message and live it among the people.

There are times when sermons seem literally to jump at Dr. Prince out of the Bible. Some of his best sermon outlines have been scribbled on the backs of envelopes in such moments, and some of his best preaching has come from these gratifying experiences. He watches at all times for things that will be useful in his preaching, gathering illustrations from his reading and from the experiences of life. He buys and reads many books but, above all, reads the Bible and gathers from it his sermonic material.*

A. E. Prince, Jr.

Dr. Prince's only son. "Junior" insisted on having his picture taken with his Bible in hand.

---

* Dr. Prince has had two libraries. He disposed of approximately 3,500 books when he left for New Zealand. He has built a second library, about as large, since he returned from overseas.

X.

STILL GOING ON

The inspiring thing about Dr. Prince is that he is still going on. The years have dealt kindly with him. He steadfastly refuses to retire. He regards his commission to preach as a life-time assignment and the churches seem to agree with him because he is never idle so much as one Sunday. He is an inspiration to all of us younger men.

Preaching

Beyond any question, God has abundantly blessed the preaching of Dr. Prince. The man is versatile and has a message suited to his congregation—whether on a street corner or in a small country or village church, or in some large church in the Southern Baptist Convention, or far away overseas—always and everywhere the Lord has blessed his work. All down the long stretch of the years he has sought ever to be God's man, in God's place, at God's time, preaching God's message to dying humanity. This book would not be complete without a study of the hidings of his power. What manner of man is this who has been entrusted with the task of preaching the Gospel for more than three score years?

A Dedicated Man

First of all, he is a dedicated man. His pulpit manners as well as his daily walk before his people make this fact apparent to all. At the first session of the League of Nations, as Lord

Robert Cecil sat on the platform, a reporter looking down on him from the balcony wrote these words: "He seems to be a dedicated man." Such has been the impression given others by Dr. Prince as evidenced by an outstanding theologian in the following letter. Dr. Penrose St. Amant, now the Dean of Theology, and David T. Porter, Professor of Church History at the Southern Baptist Seminary, Louisville, Kentucky, was a student in Louisiana College when Dr. Prince began his pastorate there. On the occasion of Dr. Prince's fiftieth anniversary celebration, Dr. St. Amant wrote him the following letter:

> "I vividly remember that September Sunday in 1934 when I saw you for the first time. It was the first Sunday after my return to Louisiana College after the summer vacation. I was in the congregation when you came out to preach. I did not even know who you were because I had not learned that Dr. Gayer, the former pastor, had resigned while I was away in the summer. You struck me immediately as a man of deep dedication but also as a man of sympathy, kindness and understanding. The years I have known you since have confirmed this initial judgment. I shall, of course, never forget the revival meeting you preached in the church in Pineville which swept the Louisiana College campus with a fervor and power which left a lasting impression upon all of us. It stands alone and unique in my religious experience.
>
> Much more could be said but I shall be content with a simple but sincere word of appreciation for giving me my start as a teacher when you asked me to come to Hannibal-LaGrange College in 1942. I shall always remember you with deep appreciation and great gratitude."

Even so, wherever he is seen, Dr. Prince always appears to be a dedicated man. In fact, we younger men feel that whenever Dr. Prince rises up, heaven comes down.

A Preacher of the Word

In the second place, he is a man of the Book. When Sir Walter Scott was dying he said to his servant, "Bring me the

Book." The frightened servant asked: "What book?" Scott replied: "There is but one Book—the Bible." Throughout the history of the Christian religion, the world's great preachers have always made much use of the Bible in their preaching. God's word to Jonah was, "Go—unto that great city, and preach unto it the preaching that I bid thee." The message of the true preacher is hewn out of the solid rock of God's eternal Word, and woe betide the preacher who is not willing to work long at that quarry. "Preach the Word" is God's solemn challenge to every preacher.

For more than threescore years, Dr. Prince has been pre-eminently a preacher of the Word of God. His preaching has been greatly influenced by the text of a sermon he heard at the beginning of his ministry: "We preach not ourselves, but Christ Jesus the Lord, and ourselves your servants for Jesus' sake." The spoken word is still a mighty weapon on the lips of the men who faithfully preach it. The world's greatest churches have been built by great preaching. Shortly before his death, Dr. Mark A. Matthews said: "Eighty-five per cent of the pulpits of America have lost the emphasis on the key-notes of the Gospel." Is it any wonder that we have come to such a time of national decay?

A Humble Man

There is no braggadocio about Dr. Prince. The theme of his entire ministry might be summed up in these words of Paul: "God forbid that I should glory, save in the cross of our Lord Jesus Christ." Again and again he quotes these words:

> "In the cross of Christ I glory,
> Towering o'er the wrecks of time;
> All the light of sacred story
> Gathers round its head sublime."

One of his favorite texts is: "Unto me, who am the least of all saints, is this grace given, that I should preach." He often reads the second chapter of First Corinthians, and after the example of Paul, he moves among his people "in weakness, and in fear, and in much trembling," preaching "not with enticing words of man's wisdom, but in demonstration of the Spirit and of power," to the end that the faith of his people "should not stand in the wisdom of men, but in the power of God."

He asks no greater joy than to be allowed to stand in humility at the foot of the line when all of God's preachers are stood in line, counting it a gladness above all gladnesses that he is permitted to have the lowliest place. He is often heard quoting these words:

"I'd rather be the least of them
Who are the Lord's alone;
Than wear a royal diadem
And sit upon a throne."

It is significant to note that he has never before permitted anyone to write his biography because in his opinion there is nothing worth the writing. He has never sought public office, neither has he sought the praise of men. He could have filled well the highest office in the gift of his brethren, but he shunned such office and was content to be one of God's noblemen in the rear ranks. Humility adorns him as doth a garment.

A Man of Prayer

Dr. Prince was called at 4:00 a.m. on a sub-zero wintry day to hasten across town to the bedside of a devout Christian woman who was dying. When he entered the room all the relatives were there and one by one she was taking each of them by the hand and speaking her gracious words of farewell. When she had finished, she turned to her pastor who was standing beside the bed, and said: "Pastor, I have sent for you because I want to hear you pray once more before I go home to be with the Lord." Dr. Prince was at that time in his mid-thirties. He states that as he prayed beside that bed, as the fingers of dawn were streaming across the sky, it seemed to him and others that they just walked on and on toward heaven until they wondered if they would ever come back or just go on home and be with the Lord.

This was a transforming experience for the young pastor. Since that time he has had many similar experiences. There has been something about his prayers that has caused even the dying to want to tarry to hear him pray once more before they go home to heaven. The people who have made these requests have probably never known what a blessing came to the pastor because of their requests.

Dr. Prince insists that his prayer life is poor and unworthy, but that his experiences have convinced him of the need of a greater prayer life. He has walked with God in most intimate prayer relationship, and looking up from his work many times during the day, he has breathed out his prayer into the ear of a loving and prayer-answering God. He anoints his plans, his sermons, his pastoral duties, and all of life's relationships with most earnest prayer.

A Shepherd's Heart

Like his Lord and Master, he looks upon the multitudes with compassion. He cannot watch a parade pass by without being probed to the depths of his heart by the thought of the large number of lost people on the march. He is never happier than when he is doing something for others. He has seemed to his people to be just one of the family in every home. His heart is strongly touched by the sufferings of others. He will not conduct a funeral unless he can take the sorrow of the bereaved to his own heart and feel that their sorrow is his sorrow, and can truthfully say with the old-time prophet: "I sat where they sat." This has made him much-sought-after for funerals and especially by people baffled and broken by the trials and temptations of life.

A Busy Man

God always calls busy men. There is no place for drones in the Lord's work. Dr. Prince has always carried at least two jobs at the same time throughout his ministry. He has always been a hard working man. On the occasion of his fiftieth anniversary he received two letters from dear friends which indicate how his busy life looked to these great men.

Dr. J. Norris Palmer, for nearly four decades Pastor of the First Baptist Church, Baton Rouge, Louisiana, and former President of the Louisiana Baptist Convention, wrote the following letter:

> I remember quite vividly your magnificent work for our denomination while you were also serving so well as pastor of the Pineville First Church. It seemed to me that you must never have spent an idle moment. If you were not busy with your pastorate or with your duties as president of our State Executive Board you were in a revival meeting or otherwise making some outstanding contribution to the cause of Christ. Then came your same sort of zealous service elsewhere in our State, followed by your great success in Missouri.
>
> Your continued tireless service beyond retirement has been an inspiration to me. It was a joy to learn in Honolulu last summer how much you are appreciated there and of your having been asked to return to work in that city. We were glad to see you take the position you have just left at Lafayette, and we are sorry you are no longer there."

Dr. Millard Jenkins, for almost a generation pastor of the First Baptist Church, Abilene, Texas, and one of Dr. Prince's cherished friends, wrote the following congratulatory letter for the fiftieth annivesary:

> "Congratulations beyond words to express for the noble, far-visioned and ever successful ministry that has crowned your labors in so many different fields.
>
> As one of the Lord's travelers "who went about doing good," your 2,500,000 miles place you at the head of the list. As teacher, many are the students who sat at your feet, rise up to call you blessed. As an executive, four schools you served as president, declare your worth. As a pastor and evangelist, your 10,000 conversions and 15,000 additions to the churches, together with your 15,000 sermons preached tell of one who magnified his ministry every day, counted time by heart throbs, mastered all circumstances that would have hindered the work of the Kingdom of God.
>
> Our fellowship in the Lord and His glorious work in past years, remain with me as a joyful memory. May our paths meet again."

The Pulpit is his Throne

He has ever held the highest regard for the pulpit of any and all churches. To him it is the most sacred spot on earth. He recalls that when he was a lad, he was secretary of the Sunday School in a rural church. It was customary to read the report for the day at the close of the Sunday School. He stood to read his report one Sunday with one foot on the floor and the other on the pulpit platform, and afterward suffered considerable remorse over the fact that it might not be proper for him to touch the pulpit. He has in the living room of his home the old pulpit desk behind which his father stood and preached on the day he was converted seventy years ago, and reverentially regards this as his choicest possession.

Dr. E. Stanley Jones delivered an address some years ago to preachers only in the First Baptist Church, Dallas, Texas. After the message there was a question and answer period for the hundreds of preachers present. One earnest preacher asked: "Dr. Jones, how can I have just the atmosphere of worship I want when I enter my pulpit to preach on Sunday morning?" Dr. Jones replied: "Take it there." This one statement has transformed the study habits, the prayer life, and the pulpit demeanor of Dr. Prince. It transforms a pulpit from an often crude something in the end of a building, to a throne from which imperial tidings are issued to dying, judgment-bound men. The quality of any man's preaching will be colored by his inmost regard for the pulpit from which he speaks. To Dr. Prince, his pulpit is preeminently his throne, and he seeks to build a high regard for it in the hearts of his people by maintaining in his own heart, and in his demeanor, the highest and most sacred regard for it.

ILLUSTRATIONS

Some one has said that illustrations are as windows to a sermon. Happy is the preacher who can use them skillfully. We are happy to present some of the illustrations which Dr. Prince uses from time to time.

Good News

Alfred Tennyson once asked an aged Methodist woman what was in the news. The old Christian replied: "Why, Mr. Tennyson, there's only one piece of news that I know—that Christ died for all men." Mr. Tennyson said to her: "That is old news, and good news, and new news." This is the only news for our broken-hearted, sinning, suffering, and dying humanity. All the good news of the glorious Gospel of Christ can be summed up in one matchless statement: "Christ died for our sins."

Preach to Troubled Hearts

The earnest words of counsel of an aged, dying preacher to the young ministers at his bedside were these: "Preach to troubled hearts. Many in your congregation have suffered losses and their hearts are heavy. They are looking for comfort. Don't forget to put something in your message for their troubled hearts."

Trusted With Sorrows

An old Christian mother who had lost her husband and most of her children was asked what period of her life she had enjoyed most on her long journey and she said—"The hours when my loved ones went away were the best of all, for Christ was so near to me and I learned so much from Him." Someone said to her: "The Lord must love you because He has trusted you with so much sorrow."

A Better House

A man and his wife were driving along the highway when, on rounding a curve, they came suddenly on a group of children playing in the road. The children scampered to safety, but left some of their playthings in the road. In spite of the driver's efforts to avoid it, the car struck a small toy playhouse and crushed it, and as he drove on he could see through the mirror of his car the little girl crying over her broken playhouse. The man could not sleep that night; the following morning, having purchased a new and better toy playhouse he drove out and gave it to the little girl. Sometime later the man was dying. Calling his wife to his bedside, he reminded her of the incident and said: "My house is being broken now, and I know that God will not do less for me than I did for the little girl——He will give me a better house."

At the Western Gate

Life's greatest adventure is at the Western Gate. Men have looked in that direction from the days of Abel and have asked many questions as to what lies beyond the sunset. The Christian religion has done much to dwindle down that ugly thing we call "death." When Dr. A. J. Gordon, long-time pastor of Clarendon Street Baptist Church, entered into rest, Dr. A. T. Pierson was called at 3:00 a.m. and asked to conduct the funeral service. At the service Dr. Pierson told that after he received this call he was not able to sleep more that night and began reading his Greek New Testament to see what it really said about death. He finished reading it through by the time of the funeral and stated that he was surprised to find that after the Resurrection of Jesus the Apostles avoided the use of the word "death" to express the departure of a Christian. Instead, they used such metaphors as "die in the Lord," "Fallen asleep," "At Home with the Lord," "Asleep in Jesus," and "Forever with the Lord."

Joint Heirs

We are "heirs of God and joint heirs with Christ." A "joint heir" can receive his inheritance only on condition that the other "joint heir" also receives his inheritance. Therefore, our inheritance is as sure and as secure as the inheritance of Jesus.

Kipling's Want

Our supreme need is the need of God. On Rudyard Kipling's last visit to America he was very seriously ill in San Francisco. The crisis hour drew near. The physician came late in the evening, and, after examining his patient, he told the nurse that the crisis would come that night and warned that the slightest disturbance might prove fatal to the distinguished patient. As the hours of the night slowly passed the nurse moved with noiseless steps as she ministered to him. After a time she saw the lips of the patient moving and stooped to listen. She heard him whisper the words, "I want," and presently again the words, "I want." The nurse feared to speak lest the sound of her voice should shock the patient, but after some time she ventured to whisper gently, "What do you want?" The great man whispered, "I want God." This is what the soul wants in every hour of crisis, and especially at the brink of the River beyond which lies the mysterious land of the unending Tomorrow.

Remembering Our Fall

Jerome states that Peter fell upon his knees every time he heard a chicken crow after he had denied his Lord and had been restored to fellowship. Our repentance may be genuine and our restoration to fellowship may be complete, but we must ever afterwards live with the fact that there was a time when that fellowship was broken and that it was our fault.

The Red Spot

Napoleon looked over the map of the world. England was colored red on the map. Napoleon said: "If it weren't for that red spot I would conquer the world." If it weren't for Calvary, sin would conquer the world, but the world will not hear of Calvary unless God's people give the Gospel to the world.

A Teacher's Devotions

Years ago a group of students, prompted by a desire to look in on the prayer habits of their old teacher of theology, stood in the darkness under his open window while he was having his devotions before going to bed. He read aloud various choice portions of Scripture until the clock struck ten and then, closing his Bible, folded his hands over it and, looking heavenward, said: "Lord, I thank Thee that we are on the same good old terms as before." To that dear teacher, God was right there all the time and he could pour out his own soul to Him on most familiar terms for his bed-time prayer. This is the heritage of all who "dwell in the secret place of the Most High, and abide in the shadow of the Almighty."

Three Inscriptions

Over each of the triple doors of the Cathedral of Milan is found an inscription. Over the first door is inscribed the words: "All that pleases is but for a moment." Over the second door is a cross and these words: "All that troubles is but for a moment." Over the third door is this inscription: "That only is important which is eternal."

Too Late

During the time of William III, Northern Scotland was in revolt. The king offered to pardon all the rebels who would take the oath of allegiance within a prescribed time. Chief MacIan, of one of the leading clans, said: "I will take the oath, but I want to be the last one to take it." He purposely delayed to start until he had just enough time to reach the imperial city before the zero hour. A great storm arose and snow packed the roads and rendered travelling almost impossible. He started, but started too late. He arrived, but arrived too late. His life was the price of his delay.

How to Preach Commandments

A young preacher asked an elderly preacher how to preach on the Ten Commandments. The elderly preacher said: "If your congregation is poor, preach these as commands; if middle class, as requests; if more affluent, as suggestions." There is only one way to preach the commandments, and that is as commands. They are introduced with the statement: "And God spoke all these words."

Where John Knox Prayed

Dr. J. B. Gambrell once made a good will tour of Europe for Southern Baptists. He visited the church in which John Knox had preached. The caretaker was showing him around the building and presently came to a small room having one door, one window, one chair, and one table. The caretaker said: "This was the prayer room of John Knox." They entered the room and the caretaker pointed to two grooves in the floor where the boards were about worn through. The caretaker said: "This is where John Knox put his knees when he prayed." Dr. Gambrell said: "Stand aside, man! Let me put my knees where John Knox put his knees when he prayed." The prayer room of John Knox sent forth streams of influence that shook the world, and any other prayer room can do as much when it contains a soul that will pray. It is said that the knees of John Knox were calloused like the knees of a camel.

Immortalized by One Act

Some years ago a United States battleship was sent to Tunis, Africa, to take up the body of a man who had been buried there for some years and to bring that body to America. When the ship returned to the harbor in New York, the body was taken to Washington and down Pennsylvania Avenue, "The Avenue of Presidents," and was laid to rest with the nation's illustrious dead. The man who was so signally honored had done but one thing to immortalize his name. He was sitting on the curb of the street in Paris, France, homeless, friendless and penniless. He took from his pocket an old envelope and wrote a hymn on the back of it that will be sung as long as our civilization endures. The man was John Howard Payne, and the hymn was "Home, Sweet Home."

Shall We Meet Again?

A young Greek hero was led forth to execution, marching under a blazing summer sun. The girl of his heart stepped out from the throng of onlookers that lined the road and walked beside him. As they walked along, she asked: "Shall we meet again?" He replied: "I asked that question of the hills, that seem eternal; of the streams, which flow on forever; of the stars, in whose azure field my raised spirit roamed in glory; these are all dumb, but as I look into your eyes I feel that there must be something in your love that will never perish: we shall meet again."

The Age of Reason

It is said that Tom Paine sent the manuscript of "The Age of Reason" to Benjamin Franklin before publishing it and asked Franklin's advice about the publication of it. Franklin wrote: "Do not turn this tiger loose. If our people are what they are now with the Bible, what will they be without it?" But Paine did turn it loose, and later when he came to die he said: "I would give worlds, if I had them, if the "Age of Reason" had never been written." The nurse who attended him in his dying hours said: "All the wealth of Europe is not enough to engage me to attend another dying infidel."

Daniel Webster's Goal

When Daniel Webster entered college someone asked him what he intended to make of himself, and he replied: "First of all, I must make of myself a man."

Resolutions of Jonathan Edwards

Jonathan Edwards wrote in his diary "Resolved, first of all, that every man should live always and everywhere at his highest and best for God. Resolved, secondly, that whether any other man in all the world strives to do so or not, I will, so help me God." Because of his adherence to these strong words, the name of Jonathan Edwards will live as long as our Christian civilization shall endure.

Sins Come Home

I stood one day in the office of an eye specialist, a member of my church. He had just examined the eyes of a bright and beautiful little girl. The physician told the parents that the little girl would be blind before she grew to womanhood. The pale and trembling father said: "Doctor, my life was not all it should have been in my youth. Can that be the cause?" The physician said, "You needed not to have told me. Certainly that is the cause of your child's approaching blindness."

When Coolidge Became President

When President Harding died suddenly on the west coast, all eyes searched for Vice-President Coolidge. He was found far out in the country at the home of his father in Vermont. A thrill went through the nation as people were told how President Coolidge, with his hand on the old family Bible, and by the light of a kerosene lamp, took the oath of office administered by his father, who was a notary. The praying people of America rejoiced when they read that in the first gleam of morning light, and before the secret service men who were racing at dangerous speed to reach and guard the president, could arrive, Coolidge slipped away to the little cemetery and knelt by his mother's grave and promised his mother he would faithfully perform the duties of his high office. There is hope for a land with such a president. It is significant and should be noted here that no mark of shame ever marred the crystal record of the Coolidge administration—neither in his private life, in his family, or in his public service. God give us men like him!

Spiritual Leaders

Roger W. Babson once said: "Today the nation is in another unemployment pocket. As Whitefield pulled us out following 1730; as Finney saved the day following 1810; as Moody reshaped America beginning in 1856; and as scores of national evangelists restored confidence following 1898, so the nation is awaiting such spiritual leaders today."

Gypsy Smith

Gypsy Smith was one of the world's successful evangelists. A certain preacher approached him to ask him the secret of his success. Among other questions, the preacher asked Gypsy Smith the best method to start a revival. Smith replied: "Brother, go back home, lock yourself up in a private room. Take a piece of chalk and mark a circle on the floor. Get down on your knees inside the circle, and pray God to start a revival inside that circle. Stay there until the prayer is answered and you will find that the revival is on."

MY GOLDEN PASTORATE

By A. E. PRINCE

The pastorate at Immanuel Baptist Mission ended with a unanimous call from Maplewood Park Baptist Church, East St. Louis, to serve as interim pastor. I began work there on Sunday, January 3, 1960. The subject of my first serman was "Carry On" (Phil. 3:12-13), and this was the theme of all my ministry there. There were 492 in Sunday School, 139 in Training Union, 351 in Morning Worship, 157 in the Evening Worship, and an offering of $838.45 for the day. There was one addition for baptism and five by letter, and thus began another happy pastorate. I have asked Pastor Bryant to allow me to write this chapter because I want to pay tribute to this wonderful church.

I had gone to serve as interim pastor for a period not to exceed three months, but like all my interim pastorates, save one, this extended beyond anticipated terminal date. The pulpit committee made several trips and held many meetings and finally came to urge me to take the pastorate. I refused for some time to yield to the request but finally, on May 4, 1960, I was unanimously called as pastor. I had no idea at that time that I would be there for more than six years. The Lord has His own plans for our lives and if we yield to Him in all things, He will lead us to see that His way is best.

Let no one from any other church I have served feel that

I am prejudiced when I refer to my pastorate at Maplewood Park as *My Golden Pastorate*. It is the pastorate of my golden years—the late afternoon of life. This was a pastorate to which God led me by an unusual pathway and for unusual purposes. This good church needed just what God enabled me to supply. The glory of the Lord went before me and God gave me the hearts of the people. I went to every task armed with the conviction that God placed me there. This conviction was shared by the people in the church and those of the community round about. When we met to worship the power of the Lord came down and we knew that God was among His people.

The church needed everything. They had moved from the old building beside the railroad to the present location—Range Lane at Howell Avenue. Pastor H. C. Croslin and the men of the congregation had worked many hours—and often far into the night—trying to erect a place of worship. They first worshipped in what is now the dining room. Later on they completed what is now the educational unit. The people were poor and times were hard and money scarce. The men gave their time and worked many times to point of exhaustion. No one can ever forget those days and their sacrificial service. As soon as possible the worship services were moved from what is now the dining room to the large and much more commodious room on the west side of the educational building. Equipment was scarce and the pinch of poverty was felt in every department and classroom of the building. There is not a room in the whole building that has not been given added equipment or repairs, little by little as we could afford it.

During the fall of 1960 we put emphasis on stewardship and observed Demonstration Day on November 13th, with pledges totaling $44,000.00 in one day. This was an all time record for Maplewood Park Baptist Church.

About this time I started a campaign to raise money to purchase an organ. This was not a church movement but an appeal to individuals who wanted to contribute to an organ fund. The money was raised, the organ installed, and a dedicatory service held at the Sunday evening service, October 15, 1961. Mrs. Herbert Schmitz was the first organist and she served until she and her family moved away.

On Thanksgiving Day, November 23, 1961, at 9:30 a.m. we had a Thanksgiving Service in our church; and having such a service became a custom observed annually during the remainder of my pastorate.

One innovation of my administration was the change of time of our Sunday evening service from 7:30 p.m. to 5:00 p.m. This was done on the recommendation of the pastor and has continued until this time.

I did not hold as many revivals as I have usually held in my churches, nor did I go out for many revivals in other churches. I stayed close to home and we maintained a perennial revival with additions about every Sunday. The greatest revival in the history of the church was held March 4 - 11, 1962. Rev. H. R. Northcutt of Waterloo, Illinois did the preaching and Rev. Verne Ballard led the singing. There were 77 professions of faith on the last Sunday, and 38 additions by letter. There were additions at every service. I baptized 50 people on Wednesday night after the revival services closed. This was the largest number ever baptized at one time in the history of the church. A spirit of revival prevailed the year around. Almost six hundred people united with the church during my pastorate.

In the spring of 1962 a movement was started to build an auditorium. Dr. Noel M. Taylor, Executive Secretary of the Illinois Baptist State Association, helped me lay plans and secure a loan of $140,000.00 in Broadway Bonds which were sold in a short time. Mr. Walter Kromm and associates were the architects, and Joe Naylor of our church was the contractor. An indebtedness of approximately $33,000.00 was paid off and approximately $115,000.00 was spent in erecting a new auditorium in the summer and fall of 1963.

Ground Breaking Service

On Sunday, March 17, 1963, at 2:30 p.m. a ground breaking service was held. A large congregation assembled at the church and listened to a stirring message delivered by Rev. Bill Fox, Pastor of State Street Baptist Church of East St. Louis. At the close of this service the congregation assembled in the churchyard for the ground breaking. John Fisher had brought a plow from his farm and a long cable was attached to it. The men of the church held the cable and pulled the plow while the pastor held the plow handles, and thus the ground was broken.

Joe Naylor

Construction began the following morning under the direction of Joe Naylor, one of our best men. Too much good cannot be said about Joe. He was not a "straw boss" standing around and giving orders. He worked beside the men using his hammer and saw. He worked not only all day long, but often for hours in the night when all others were gone. He built the pulpit now used in the church. He painted the picture in the baptistry. His whole life was wrapped up in the church building program. He refused a contractor's pay and accepted only a carpenter's check. He was a trustee of the church, assistant Sunday School Superintendent, and held other offices in the church.

Joe passed away September 21, 1965 at Centerville Hospital following a heart attack. The funeral sermon was preached by

Ground breaking, Maplewood Park Baptist Church, East St. Louis, Sunday afternoon, March 17, 1963.

Since Dr. Prince found out what carpenters get an hour I believe he's hintin'

In addition to his skills as contractor, carpenter, and painter, Joe Naylor found time to demonstrate his ability as cartoonist. He drew the cartoon above as a "take-off" on Dr. Prince.

the pastor on September 24, 1965 in the Maplewood Park Auditorium, which he had erected; and he was laid to rest beside his daughter, Barbara, in Lakeview Memorial Cemetery.

The First Service

The first service held in the new auditorium was on Thanksgiving Day, November 28, 1963. The building was not completed but could be used for the service. More than 300 people were present. The first Sunday services in the new sanctuary were held on Sunday, December 22, 1963. The building was formally dedicated on Sunday, January 5, 1964. Rev. L. H. Moore preached at 10:45 a.m., and the dedicatory sermon was preached by Dr. Noel M. Taylor at 2:30 p.m. Rev. H. C. Croslin, former pastor, preached at 5:00 p.m. This was a day of rejoicing by the people.

On Sunday, January 12, a surprise was planned for the pastor celebrating the sixtieth anniversary of his work in the ministry. He was not aware of this plan until Tommie Hopewell, Chairman of Deacons, took charge of the morning service and presented the pastor with a diamond-studded lapel button having the figure 60 on it. An address was delivered by Dr. O. M. McCann, a lifelong friend of the Pastor, and the anniversary sermon was preached by Rev. L. L. Leininger, longtime friend of the pastor. The surprise for the pastor continued at the noon hour when he was led to a meal served in the church dining room. An open house reception for the pastor and his wife was held in the afternoon from 2:00 to 4:00 P.M. The pastor preached at 5:00 P.M. It was a very bad day without, with much snow, but a delightful day within among the people.

Two years later, and at the close of my pastorate, the church gave me a gold diamond-studded pin with the figure 62 on it in commemoration of my 62 years of service in the ministry.

The pin was attached to my lapel by Pastor Carvin Bryant at the 5:00 P.M. service Sunday, March 27, 1966. The anniversary sermon was delivered by Rev. Arthur E. Farmer, Assistant Executive Secretary of the Executive Board of the Illinois Baptist State Association.

Faithful Workers

The victories of these eventful years are not won by one man. The preaching of the Gospel is important and a fundamental necessity for the progress of any spiritual movement. But the people had a mind to work. Maplewood Park Baptist Church has in its membership a great number of people who put their church first in all their working and planning and giving. And the combined work of all, and the prayers of all striving together in the fellowship of the Gospel of Christ, and all this undergirded by faithful preaching and holy living, is the secret of the achievements of those six years.

Who can forget the years of labor of Sue Hawkins for our young people? She has given of her time and talent and has made one of the largest contributions to the welfare of our young people and for the success of the program of the church. She has steadfastly refused to accept pay for her work with the choir. It is a labor of love on her part. Only eternity can reveal the full measure of the results of her work. And throughout my years of service there, Joe Hawkins has served in an admirable manner as chairman of ushers and no church has had more efficient usher service than Maplewood Park. Blessings on these good people.

Time and space fail us when we think of all others whose sacrificial service and undying devotion has made possible great advances in the work of the church. One thinks of Rev. Verne Ballard who came during my first year and served so faithfully and helpfully for three years, followed in this office of music director by Bill Hanks, and Everett Lee Foy. And who can forget the service rendered by Mrs. Pat Lockhart, an experienced nursery worker, who has tansformed our nursery, and we now have one of the best in this area. And Mrs. McKindley, known to her friends as "Cookie," has served hundreds of meals, to few or multitudes, as no one else has ever done for us. All this service she has rendered without compensation. There will be a great reward in heaven for her. There is the Brotherhood prayer meeting at 7:00 A.M. on Sunday which has been maintained for four years. These men have started the day right each Sunday morning by an hour of prayer. And the faithful deacons, trustees, Brotherhood and W.M.U. members, Sunday School and Training Union workers and members—if only time and space permitted us to name hundreds of these and tell of their exploits. Surely the Lord was with us every step of the way.

Mention must be made of the kindergarten movement started one year ago. Much credit for the great success of this movement goes to Rev. Sherman D. Bridgeman, our City Missionary, who is a member of our church and Chairman of the Kindergarten Committee. Many men gave hours of labor to prepare the nursery and kindergarten space in the old auditorium. What a mighty army of workers!

I must pay tribute to those faithful workers who were fellow-laborers with me in the church office. Mrs. Betty Laxton has given much of her life to Maplewood Park Baptist Church. I knew Betty when she was a little girl playing with my children in the parsonage yard when I was pastor at Eldorado, Illinois. She was in the office of Maplewood Park Baptist Church when I began work there, and is still serving in a very efficient manner.

Mrs. Jeanette Parker served for quite some time before moving to Arizona. On her return she began work in the church office and is a very faithful and efficient helper. The Parker family were given a royal welcome on their return from the West.

We had with us for three years Rev. Verne Ballard and family. Brother Ballard was converted in Maplewood Park Church when his father was pastor here. Verne was the capable and dedicated music director of our church and wrought a great work in our midst. Mrs. Ballard also served in various places in our church. We suffered a great loss when the Ballard family left us. We had with us at various times Ima Brandt, Sue Hawkins, Martha Wood, Brenda Brandt, Nancy Batson, Elaine Royal, Janet O'Connor, and others of whom the world is not worthy, and time and space forbids mention of many others. May the Lord reward them, each and all.

Then—the library. Mildred Gaither took over this work soon after I went to Maplewood Park. She has worked faithfully and built up a wonderful church library. She is a skilled librarian and has developed the library in a wonderful way. It certainly is a joy to have such a library and such a librarian.

Pastor Bryant Called

All good things come to an end, and pastorates should come to an end. I have always felt that a pastor ought to resign—if for no other reason, to at least give the church a chance to get another man. Without consulting anyone about the matter, and after days of soul-agony as I contemplated the matter, I surprised my dear congregation by announcing on Sunday, October 24, 1965, that I would close my work as of January 2, 1966. So far as I know, there was not a member of the church who wanted a change in pastors. The announcement was hard to make and came as a distinct shock to the people. There were many tears shed in the days that followed—and lots of them by the preacher and his lovely wife. It is hard to take this step

Sixty-second anniversary of Dr. Prince's ministry at Maplewood Park Baptist Church, 1965. Pastor Carvin C. Bryant pins 62 year pin on Dr. Prince's lapel while Rev. Arthur Farmer, who preached the anniversary sermon, looks on.

and we have not recovered from it even yet. Rev. Carvin C. Bryant, Pastor of Clarendon Hills Baptist Church, Chicago, and President of the Illinois Baptist State Association, was called to the pastorate and expected to begin his work in January, but he and his family were in a car wreck on their way to Maplewood Park and he and Mrs. Bryant were in the hospital for quite some time, and he was not able to begin his work until March. So this poor preacher carried on until he was able to take over, thus extending his period of service to about six years and three months.

Pastor Bryant took full charge of the work the last of March. He is a great preacher and a devoted pastor and he and his good family have been royally welcomed to our church. My membership is still there. Pastor Bryant and I have an agreement. He is my pastor, and I am his pastor, by his choice, and never has there been a more cordial relationship between a pastor and his predecessor. So far we haven't tried to borrow money from each other!

Thank God for Pastor Bryant and Maplewood Park Baptist Church. Everything goes better after I leave a church. They have even paved Mildred Avenue "since I left."

Dr. Prince says that in the early years of his ministry, he had hoped to become a great preacher, but that in these later years he hopes that some youth whose life he touches may become all that he dreamed that he would be as he assessed his life in those early years. During the time we have worked together on this book he has again and again expressed the prayerful wish that the book may fall into the hands of some young people who are facing decisions leading to a great field of service for God. Such young people are the constant burden of his prayers as this book is sent forth to earnest readers.

We will not know until the books are opened at the judgment of God just how far the influence of this book will extend, nor how many who read it may find God's will for their lives and God's place of service for them. To God be all the glory!

SIXTIETH ANNIVERSARY

The Sixtieth Anniversary of the ministry of Dr. Prince was celebrated by the deacons and members of Maplewood Park Baptist Church on Sunday, January 12, 1964. This came as a complete surprise to him. The deacons took over the morning service. Dr. O. M. McCann, lifelong friend, delivered an address, and Rev. L. L. Leininger preached the anniversary sermon. To the surprised pastor was given a diamond-studded pin having the number 60 on it. A dinner was served in the church dining room and an open house held in the afternoon in his honor.

Dr. Prince has a number of anniversaries in December and January. The anniversary of his birth, his conversion, his reception into church membership, his call to preach, his first sermon, his license to preach—all occur in these two months. Letters of congratulations poured into the office of Maplewood Park Church on this anniversary celebration. We present herewith some of them.

REV. L. H. MOORE, EDITOR
Illinois Baptist

It is a real pleasure for me to have this opportunity of extending my personal greetings to you on this occasion of your anniversaries.

I am especially grateful for the privilege of having fellowship with you and sharing a few days with you in your church. I have long appreciated your many abilities and respected you in your dedication and accomplishments, but "the half was not told me." You are a preacher after the likeness of Spurgeon, a friend in the similitude of Jonathan, a doughty warrior in the tradition of Caleb, but, most of all, a warmhearted Gospel preacher who knows and loves the Lord Jesus. I like you because you "cover the ground where you stand."

DR. NOEL M. TAYLOR
Executive Secretary
Illinois Baptist State Association

I count it a privilege and joy to join with a host of othei friends of yours in honoring you on the occasion of the Sixtieth Anniversary of your ministry. I know of no one among Southern Baptists in Illinois (and very few if any beyond Illinois) who has had as rich and varied experiences in the ministry as you.

You were preaching in 1907 when the Illinois Baptist State Association was organized. You have seen the development of our Southern Baptist work here in the State all through the years. You have served as pastor in Illinois, Missouri, Louisiana and Texas. Your pastoral experience includes churches in New Zealand and Hawaii. Your experience includes serving as head of one Baptist Academy and president of three colleges.

And now at an age when many of us will have become sour and bitter and useless, you are experiencing at Maplewood Park one of the most fruitful ministries in our entire state. I salute you and congratulate you and thank God for you.

DR. G. EARL GUINN, PRESIDENT
Louisiana College

Please permit me to join many of your friends in congratulating you upon the occasion of your 60th Anniversary as a minister of the Gospel.

Perhaps you will recall that our paths first crossed when you came to Pineville as pastor of the First Baptist Church in 1934. I shall never cease to be grateful for the impact you made upon my life during my years in College. Some of my ideas about preaching—the better ones, that is—I learned from you. You were always meticulous about your preparation.

And do you remember the wonderful revivals we had in those years? The entire College was lifted by them. I saw the power of God at work in many lives by reason of those meetings.

Through the years, including some very difficult ones, you have been a constant source of inspiration and encouragement. May God's blessings be upon you and yours.

DR. ROBERT L. LEE
Executive Secretary
Louisiana Baptist Convention

It is a delightful privilege to express hearty good wishes to you and your family on the momentous occasion celebrating your marvelous and extensive ministry. Few ministers enjoy so long a life packed with so many accomplishments. Although we do not know in detail the problems you may have endured, the burdens you have borne, or the full measure of your victories, we find it difficult to imagine that you have ever failed in a Christian task set for yourself.

Preacher of the Gospel, teacher of the Word, Christian statesman, wise administrator, evangelist with many proofs of successful witnessing, promoter, and missionary—you have distinguished yourself, dear friend, in so many wonderful ways in serving your Lord and Master and the world in His name.

DR. PAUL SMITH
Executive Secretary
Iowa Baptist Convention

There is nothing that gives me more pleasure than to pause to drop a line in token of my abiding esteem for you, as a minister of the Gospel. I shall never forget my first meeting with you when I entered school at Ewing College, for it was through your patience, counselling, and deep concern for a boy, fresh off the farm, that gave me my real start in life. Perhaps, had it not been for you and my Godly mother, I never would have entered the ministry.

I may say that I have followed your ministry from the time I met you to the present time, with a deep sense of satisfaction. I do want you to know that you have definitely left your mark upon me, and I will never cease to thank God for your leadership and guidance.

DR. T. A. PATTERSON
Executive Secretary
Texas Baptist Convention

Never have I seen a man who had so many anniversaries all at once. May I add my congratulations to the many others you must have received. After all those years you spent in Texas in various capacities you deserve not only our congratulations but also our thanks for the foundations you laid and the seeds you planted. It is our hope that your service to God will continue to grow in effectiveness and outreach until you have reached the potential He meant you to reach.

Maplewood Park Baptist Church, Cahokia. The sanctuary (at left) was erected in 1963.

XI.

SUNSET DAYS

The ultimate test of all things is how they will look at the last. Jacob had a long and eventful life, but when he came to life's late afternoon only two words summed up the harvest of a life-time—Bethel and Rachel. Bethel was the place of his conversion. Rachel was his beloved wife. A most interesting thing about any man is his philosophy of life at sunset. The following lines reveal the philosophy with which Dr. Prince faces sunset.

"Since I Left"

Dr. A. E. Prince

We are all familiar with the caption—"Since I came!" This heads an article on the achievements of some one who is revealing the progress of his work. I prefer to write under the caption—"Since I Left!" There is a time to leave, and happy is the man who is able to recognize the signs which indicate that the time for departure has come. No doubt some churches are suffering because some one cannot read the signs. Some "Since I Came" men ought to resign to give themselves a chance to witness what happens "Since I Left!"

There was a time when I was so indiscreet as to imagine that it would be very difficult for an institution to get along without me. I have lived long enough to learn better. In fact, I may have lived a little too long, for I have learned that all the institutions I have served have fared better after I left. My work has been of the John the Baptist type.

During my pastorate at First Church, LaGrange, Missouri, fifty years ago, I kept preaching about the need of more room for the Sunday School, and also for a pastor's home. A commodious educational building and a pastor's home have been erected—since I left!

When I began my pastorate with First Church, Eldorado, Illinois in 1919, the people were worshipping in an old building and owed a large debt on it. During my administration the debt was paid and a building fund started. There is a very beautiful and adequate church building at Eldorado today, and it was built—since I left!

When I began my pastorate with First Church, Marion, Illinois, in 1921 they had a beautiful building, and comparatively new, but only about half as much room as we needed. Those good people have bought considerable land adjoining their property and have built a very beautiful and adequate educational building, and other needed buildings—all since I left!

The First Church of Brownwood, Texas, was deeply in debt when I arrived there in 1927. A new church building had just recently been finished, but needed furniture throughout the auditorium and the educational building. The debt was refinanced while I was there, to be paid in monthly installments over ten years. Fifty thousand dollars worth of equipment and furniture was bought and much alteration was made in the interior of the church building. There were approximately 1700 additions to the church while I was there. That good Church has paid off that indebtedness in five years instead of ten years, purchased several pieces of property adjoining the church, and finished other buildings—all since I left!

The First Church, Pineville, Louisiana, was greatly handicapped for lack of room when I arrived in 1934. The church was using the public school building for additional space for Sunday School and Training Union meetings. I immediately started a building fund. The work of the church prospered in every way—even in the dark years of the depression. There were about 1500 additions during my stay. The church budget grew from about $8,000 per year to approximately $50,000 per year. That good church has had four buildings erected in these later years, the last a large and beautiful sanctuary—and is acquiring more land and planning another building to accommodate the four thousand members and others who attend—and has a church budget several times larger than my largest budget there—and all this since I left!

The First Church, West Monroe, Louisiana, had a beautiful building and a large debt when I arrived in 1939. A financial plan was adopted and a building fund started. The church debt was refinanced and paid off long before the payments were all due. There were 389 additions. That church has now acquired almost a whole city block and conducted four building campaigns covering that block—and now has a church budget of about $350,000.00—all since I left!

Fifth Street Church, Hannibal, Missouri, had a beautiful but old sanctuary and limited educational space when I arrived in 1941. I started a building fund there. The work moved along in a very fine manner but room was urgently needed. There were 324 additions during my three years. Today this church has a large and commodious educational building and evidences of advancement are seen on every hand—all since I left!

There were three large brick buildings on the Campus of Hannibal-LaGrange College when I arrived in 1941—and a debt of $200,000. The outlook was dark. During my ten years there the school made fine progress. The indebtedness was liquidated, and fifteen buildings erected on the campus—only one of these was a brick building. We secured old barracks buildings and made duplex housing units for married students, a science building and a student center. This was the best we could do. Two large dormitories, a beautiful library, and a science building have been completed under the leadership of my successor, Dr. L. A. Foster—the enrollment has far surpassed all previous records, the largest classes ever to be graduated have received degrees and diplomas—and all this since I left!

I served one year as interim pastor at Effingham, Illinois, in 1951-52. These people had a new building—sanctuary and educational space—but badly needed more room. This church has bought adjoining property and erected a large educational building, and the work has prospered in every way—since I left!

The First Church, Lafayette, Louisiana, was worshipping in a large sanctuary with educational space attached but also wholly inadequate. The church purchased considerable adjoining property and has erected a very modern and well-planned educational building and contemplates other buildings—all since I left!

I have just left Maplewood Park Baptist Church. My successor, Pastor Carvin C. Bryant, is moving so rapidly that I can hardly keep in sight of his dust. Give him a little time and he will prove that I am good for churches and institutions after I leave!

After thinking the matter over I cannot recall a single instance where a church or an institution I have served has failed to have the blessing of God upon it, not only while I was there, but also—after I left! In fact, every one of

> the churches and institutions I have served has made greater progress after I left. None of us should take ourselves too seriously. We ought to give history a chance to repeat itself. One test of any man's work is its lasting qualities. If he has built well the work can stand the shock of his resignation. The man may not recover from the shock. A very good test of any man is his attitude toward the work after he leaves—especially if the work prospers.

It would seem that the best service I can render for any church or institution is to get out! Verily! If any delapidated church wants better days in the future—well just try me for a little while and see what happens—"since I left!"

FAVORITE HYMNS

It is difficult for any one to find one hymn among so many of our gospel songs that might be said to be one's favorite hymn. There are many good hymns that add much to our Christian experience as we hear them again and again.

Dr. Prince states that at his conversion, and just as the light dawned in his soul, the congregation was singing—

> "At the cross, at the cross
> Where I first saw the light,
> And the burden of my heart rolled away,
> It was there by faith I received my sight,
> And now I am happy all the day."

At the old-fashioned Saturday afternoon service when he presented himself for membership, and as he walked down the aisle, the congregation was singing—

> "Are there no foes for me to face?
> Must I not stem the flood?
> Is this vile world a friend to grace,
> To help me on to God?
>
> "Sure I must fight, if I would reign;
> Increase my courage, Lord;
> I'll bear the toil, endure the pain,
> Supported by Thy Word."

At his baptism, the old saints standing on the bank, sang—

"Jesus, keep me near the cross,
There a precious fountain,
Free to all, a healing stream,
Flows from Calvary's mountain.

"In the cross, in the cross,
Be my glory ever,
Till my raptured soul shall find
Rest beyond the river."

In the two old-fashioned revivals in the fall and early winter of 1896, one song was sung repeatedly, and this greatly touched the heart of the little boy who was seeking the Lord. It was entitled, "Then Rejoice, All ye Ransomed."

"There's rejoicing in the presence of the angels,
Over sinners coming home,
All the heavenly harpers with a mighty chorus
Now are praising 'round the throne.
"Then rejoice, all the ransomed,
Let your praises reach to heaven's highest dome,
For the dead's alive, the lost are found, and wand'rers
Now are coming, coming home."

On Sunday morning, May 29, 1904, as he and a young man—Roy Gantz, his closest friend—were driving to the ordination service of Dr. Prince, they sang together:

"Hark 'tis the Shepherd's voice I hear,
Out in the desert dark and drear,
Calling the sheep who've gone astray,
Far from the Shepherd's fold away.

"Bring them in, bring them in,
Bring them in from the fields of sin;
Bring them in, bring them in,
Bring the wandering ones to Jesus."

In his revivals, he has at times had a theme song. In the great revival at Ouachita College, Arkadelphia, Arkansas, his theme song was B. B. McKinney's—"In the Highways, In the Hedges."

"In the highways, in the hedges
In the highways, in the hedges,
In the highways, in the hedges,
I'll be somewhere working for my Lord.

"If you want me, you can find me,
If you want me, you can find me,
If you want me, you can find me,
I'll be somewhere working for my Lord."

In his great revival with Pastor E. E. Huntsberry and the First Baptist Church, West Monroe, Louisiana, his theme song was another of B. B. McKinney's great hymns, "Back to Bethel."

"Back to the Bible, the true Living Word,
Sweetest old story that ever was heard;
Back to the joy life, my soul longs to know,
Bethel is calling, and I must go."

"Back to Bethel, I must go,
Back where the rivers of sweet waters flow,
Back to the true life my soul longs to know,
Bethel is calling, and I must go."*

In a number of his revivals, he used for the invitation hymn, at every service, the spiritual birth hymn of Charlotte Eliot,

"Just as I am, without one plea,
But that Thy blood was shed for me,
And that Thou bidd'st me come to Thee,
O Lamb of God, I come, I come."

When the companion of his youth and mother of his children, went away in death at day-break on a dark Friday morning, he took refuge in that comforting hymn of John H. Newman:

"Lead, Kindly Light, a-mid the encircling gloom,
Lead Thou me on!
The way is dark, and I am far from home,
Lead Thou me on!
Keep Thou my feet, I do not ask to see,
The distant scene, one step enough for me.

---

* Copyright 1931, by Robert H. Coleman. Used by permission.

"So long Thy pow'r hath blessed me, sure it still
Will lead me on
O'er moor and fen, o'er crag and torrent, 'till
The night is gone,
And with the morn those angel faces smile,
Which I have loved long since, and lost awhile!

At the close of his last service as pastor at the First Church, Effingham, on Sunday morning, August 5, 1951, as he and Mrs. Prince stood at the altar for the farewell handclasp of their parishioners, as they left for New Zealand, the congregation sang B. B. McKinney's hymn:

"Take up thy cross and follow Me,"
I heard my Saviour say;
"I gave my life to ransom thee,
Surrender your all today."

Wherever He leads, I'll go,
Wherever He leads, I'll go,
I'll follow my Christ who loves me so,
Wherever He leads, I'll go.*

At a time when he was passing through fiery trials and driven almost to despair, he found comfort in these lines:

"There's One who can comfort when all else fails,
Jesus, Blessed Jesus;
A Saviour who saves though the foe assails,
Jesus, Blessed Jesus;
Once He traveled the way we go,
Felt the pangs of deceit and woe;
Who more perfectly then can know,
Jesus, Blessed Jesus.

"He never forsakes in the darkest hour,
Jesus, Blessed Jesus;
His arm is around us with keeping power,
Jesus, Blessed Jesus;
When we enter the Shadow-land,
When at Jordan we trembling stand,
He will meet us with outstretched hand,
This Jesus, Blessed Jesus."**

---

* Dr. B. B. McKinney's hymn, copyright, 1936 by the Baptist Sunday School Board, Nashville, Tennessee.

** Copyrighte 1906, by Charles H. Gabriel: E. O. Excell, owner

Almost everyone with whom he worked in the early years of his ministry are now gone to their eternal home. In his reflective moods he finds himself lost in contemplation of C. A. Tinsley's hymn:

"A little while and then the summer day,
When I go home;
'Tis lonesome winter now, but 'twill be May,
When I go home;
Beyond the gloom of moor and fen I see
The welcome warm of those who wait for me,
When I go home, when I go home."*

As he reflects over his journey of life, and what contribution he has made and what he leaves as a legacy to others, he turns to this thought-provoking hymn:

"Fading away like the stars of the morning,
Losing their light in its glorious sun;
Stealing away, let me thus end my journey
Only rememb'red by what I have done.

"Only the truth that in life I have spoken,
Only the seed that on earth I have sown;
These shall pass onward when I am forgotten,
Fruits of the harvest and what I have done.

"Fading away like the stars of the morning,
So, let my name be unhonored, unsung;
Here, or up yonder, I must be remember'red,
Only rememb'red by what I have done."

The reader will note that each of these hymns have marked some definite experience in his life. After all, that may be the way we get our favorite hymns.

HAPPY MAN AT EIGHTY

Two passages of Scripture come to mind at a glance at this title. "The path of the just is as the shining light, that shineth more and more unto the perfect day," and "The hoary head is a crown of glory, if it be found in the way of righteousness."

Some one has said: "In our search after God our wisdom doth consist, in our worship of God our religion doth consist, and in both of them our happiness doth consist."

Storm Jameson said: "Happiness comes of the capacity to feel deeply, to enjoy simply, to think freely, to risk life, to be needed."

W. Beran Wolfe said: "If you observe a really happy man you will find him building a boat, writing a symphony, educating his son, growing double dahlias in his garden, or looking for dinosaur eggs in the Gobi desert. He will not be searching for happiness as if it were a collar button that has rolled under the radiator. He will not be striving for it as a goal in itself. He will have become aware that he is happy in the course of living life twenty-four crowded hours of the day."

Happiness is not found when one is seeking for it. It is found within when one is too busy serving others to look for it. He who seeks happiness by changing anything but his own disposition, will waste his life in a fruitless search for it. There is but little happiness in the world because we seek it where it is not—in outward circumstances and external good, and fail to seek it where it alone dwells—in the chamber of the heart.

Dr. Prince is a happy man—happy at eighty! He is happy because he is at peace with God. He has walked with God three score and ten years, having become a Christian a few days before his tenth birthday.

He is happy because he is at peace with his fellow-men. He will not allow any one to be his enemy. He has ever had a forgiving spirit. It matters not how badly he may be abused and mistreated by others, he never allows this to cause him to think unkindly of anyone. He can pray as ardently for his enemies, if any, as for his friends. In his own heart he is at peace with all men.

He is clean in thought and word and deed. Never does he tell a shady story, or even listen to one if he can get away from it. He never indulges in profanity. He is ever a steadfast friend of all who will allow him to be so. Of Job it was said that he eschewed evil. This means that when Job perceived that something was evil he turned from it and had nothing to do with it.

He is happy in his home life. He had a wonderful companion in life's early years. She was one of the noblest of women, faithful to her husband and devoted to her home and children. Six fine children were born in this home and all of them lived to maturity. All are active Christians, and were all baptized by their father. They all married Christian companions, save one who has never married. Family worship has ever been maintained in his home. After thirty-seven years of married life, he lost his first home by the death of his wife. Three years later he married a lovely Christian woman who is the pride and joy of his heart and life in these later years. She is a highly educated and accomplished woman, an educator by profession, and an experienced church worker. Peace and love and loyalty are the Christian graces of his home, with never an unkind word or act or thought. The presence of Christ is obvious in his home.

He is a busy man. He has not taken a vacation in thirty-five years. He never misses an opportunity to do good, and never refuses a call if he can possibly include it in his schedule. He is never happier that when he has all that he can do each day. He thinks busy men are happy men.

He is happy as he reviews the past. He has a heart filled with choicest memories of service for God in an unusually varied ministry. Few men have served so well in so many fields of service. A thousand choice memories rise at midnight on sleepless nights to flood his soul with joy and peace.

Dr. Prince and his children, grandchildren, great-grandchildren, and in-laws meet once a year in a family reunion in Texas. All of his descendants and in-laws are shown above, except for four who could not attend.

He is happy as he takes the forward look. He knows more people on the other side than he knows here. All who served with him in his early years in the ministry are gone home except Dr. I. E. Lee of Carbondale. He is a pilgrim going home to his Father's house. He has no fear as he faces the future. His only concern is that God will use him down to life's last hour.

Amy Carmichael once said: "We have all eternity to celebrate victories—but only until sunset to gain them." He has held this thought before him through the years and, with Paul, can say, "I pursue onward." He has a sermon on "The Glory of Going On." His three-point outline states that the glory of going on consists in (1) A Widening Horizon, (2) An Investment of Self, (3) A Goal Undiminished at Evening Time. "At evening time it shall be light."

He is now at the age when Moses stood at the burning bush, and five years younger than Caleb was when he asked only for a very hard task. He is of the same age as was Gladstone when he was called the "Grand Old Man of England," and at the age when Tennyson wrote "Crossing the Bar." He is five years older than Abraham was when he left Haran on his immortal pilgrimage. He finds plenty of reasons to be happy at eighty.

His philosophy of life may be summed up in these words: "I remember yesterday; I have no fear of tomorrow, and I love today."

TAPS—NOT YET

Dr. Prince is not ready for "taps." He has just received a letter from his dear friend, Rev. Cecil Martin, congratulating him on his long record of service, and the letter concludes with these words: "If you continue to preach for a while longer, you may be preaching when the Lord comes." Dr. Prince says this has given him a new idea—still preaching when Jesus comes. What a glorious privilege it would be to be preaching in the pulpit when the triumphant shout of the returning Lord and Master is heard! Dr. Prince is still preaching and hoping for the dawn of God's eternal morning. The Book of Acts closes with Paul preaching—and this book closes with Dr. Prince still preaching. He has a deep conviction that he must respond to every preaching invitation. I have often wondered why. The only answer I can think of is—

"HE WAS BORN TO PREACH."

XII.

A LESSON FOR PREACHERS

Sermon by Dr. Prince

"And the word of the Lord came unto Jonah the second time, saying, Arise, go unto Nineveh, that great city, and preach unto it the preaching that I bid thee."—Jonah 3:1-2.

•

The Book of Jonah might well be called "The Book of God's Preparations." God prepared a prophet, using withal exceeding great patience. He prepared a field of labor for that prophet, a message to be preached, and a good reception for the messenger. He prepared a great fish, a gourd, a worm, and a vehement east wind. Just here is a good place for the monkey-minded philosophers who mount our pulpits to stick a pin. They have been so busy measuring the size of a fish's throat that they have overlooked the fact that this little book of four chapters says four times that "God prepared" certain things. Anything that God prepares is sufficient for the purpose for which He designed it. There is no book in which the hand of God is more clearly seen. The last doubt in the mind of the most skeptical pseudo-philosopher ought to be dissipated by the words of Jesus, who settled the question of the authenticity of the book by an immortal application of an incident in the story to himself.

A Picked Preacher

Jonah was a preacher with the background of a definite call

of God and a very impressive experience with God. These are the necessary credentials of any man who would attempt to speak God's message to a lost world. God has reserved to Himself the task of calling His ministers. There are some who are a little uncertain about their call when it first comes to them, and there are many who may wonder at times whether or not they are in the right field of service, but there was nothing like this in the case of Jonah. He was a picked preacher. God called him and told him where to preach. He held in trust a great and vitally important message for a heathen city. He tried the patience of God, turned a whole city to repentance by one direct message from heaven, and after three thrilling chapters, he retired in a rather uncomplimentary manner. There was a lot of human nature about him and he deserves more credit than he sometimes receives. The very fact that his faults are more widely discussed than his virtues qualifies him for a place in the "Amen Corner" at any preachers' meeting.

Fortunately the ministry of Jonah does not end with the booth, the gourd, the worm, and the wind. He worked only a few days but he got on the front pages of the Nineveh newspapers and the world is not yet through talking about him. He held the only revival in history which completely evangelized a whole city, and the magnitude of his work in Nineveh is seen when we note the size of the city. There were one hundred twenty thousand which knew not their right hand from their left. If this statement refers to children, as some think, it was a city of probably a million souls. Jonah brought this whole city down into the dust of repentance, and then retired hastily and got on the shelf prematurely. He either wrote his autobiography or some one wrote the sketch of his life before he died, and although it left him wishing he were dead, he still lives.

We are very much indebted to this prophet. Every preacher reads this story with consuming interest. Some people would be in total ignorance of the Bible if he had not taken the first submarine trip in the history of mankind; for their stock of Bible knowledge consists of two characters—"Jonah and the Whale." He has kept the world laughing for nearly three milleniums, and he made at least one discovery about the size of a fish which has spread gloom and consternation in the camps of speculative philosophers for many centuries. His popularity has suffered some at the hands of critics but he is neither the first nor the last preacher to lose his popularity. This fact would give him standing room at any preachers' convention.

Ministers have been very much the same the world over, regardless of the date of their ministry. Jonah had much in common with other preachers. He had a call he never sought. He had a message he did not invent. He tried to excuse himself and paid the price of his folly. He had a brief but highly successful evangelistic career. His life alternated between genuine repentance in the sea and real pouting in the booth. This alone would advance him to a seat on the platform at any preachers' convention.

A Pioneer Preacher

Jonah was a pioneer preacher. He blazed paths. We ministers of today need not take on airs. If we are tempted to flee from duty we shall not play the part of pioneers in that role. If we forget to pray in the storm we shall not be the first ministers who acted so foolishly. If fellow-travellers, and even people who know not God, happen to reprove us, it will not be the first time unregenerated men have told the preacher what he ought to be doing. If we are cast overboard we will find a company whose name is Legion ready to give us the right hand

Two important things are written about King Uzziah, among other things recorded of his life. One is, "As long as he sought the Lord, God made him to prosper," and the other is, "When he was strong, his heart was lifted up to his destruction." Just here is a lesson every preacher should learn. Jonah tells us that he prayed because of his afflction, because of his location, and because his soul fainted within him. Do not lose sight of the connection between these reasons for prayer and his attempted flight to Tarshish. He admits that God cast him into the sea and he makes no complaint about the matter. He thought the earth with her bars was about him forever. It was a time for prayer.

When the soul of Jonah fainted within him, he remembered God. This is healthy exercise for a preacher on Monday morning. It may have been Monday morning when Jonah became a passenger on the submarine. Jonah's example shows us what to do when faint—we are to remember God. The very fact that a troubled soul remembers God is good evidence that God has not forgotten that individual. When Jonah remembered the Lord he prayed. Prayer is prompted and faith is invigorated by remembering God. The greatest mercy in time of trouble is to be kept prayerful.

The mercy of God is amazing. Jonah was an object of pity at that solitary prayer meeting. He was a guilty man. He tells us that he went down to the bottom of the mountains, that the weeds were wrapped about his head, and that he thought the earth with her bars was about him forever. But Jonah found that a disobedient preacher could pray from that strange depth and that his prayer would rise unto the holy temple of God. We are never too far from God to pray so long as the golden sceptre is extended us. Jonah's prayer was answered and he was given a second chance.

A Prepared Preacher

It cannot be said too often that so great a task as the preaching of the unsearchable riches of Christ demands the best possible preparation on the part of the messenger. All honor is due to the holy men of the past generations, who have wrought a great work for God in spite of the handicaps of a limited education. God took what they had and used it for His glory, and He still does so, but this is a day which demands much preparation on the part of the preacher. The call to preach is a call to the very best possible preparation, both in scholastic training and spiritual development.

God has His own way of preparing a preacher. In fact, He has an infinite variety of ways. He called Moses to the burning bush. He met Isaiah in the Temple. He taught Jonah in the bottom of the sea. He sent Paul into Arabia and John to Patmos. Every one of these came back with a message—and it was God's message. No man is prepared to preach until God teaches him some things that are not listed in the schools of men. The course God offers is not finished even in a life-time. The horizon of Jonah's life was pushed back in every direction when God taught him.

A Prevailing Preacher

What greater joy ever comes to a preacher than the joy he knows when his soul is intoxicated with victory? How glorious it is to see multitudes of people brought under the spell of the message of God! The revival in Nineveh is without parallel in the history of preaching. The people of that city, from the king to the humblest subject, cried mightily unto God. Men and beasts were clothed in sackcloth, which is ever the symbol of contrition, sorrow, and repentance. The repentance of these people was deep and abiding and prevailing, and stands as a rebuke to the tearless, meaningless, and easy-going so-called repentance of today. Things always happen when God's message is preached by God's messenger.

Jonah is the only preacher on record who turned a whole city to God with one message. Just here is found one of the most thrilling stories in all the history of evangelism. Jonah was faithful in declaring the message of God, and was permitted to see "results" that many preachers would like to report to the papers. He preached with prevailing power. His message was very simple, but God was in the message and the whole city was swept by the power of God. He prevailed with the people because he prevailed with God.

A Pouting Preacher

A pouting preacher is a common, though sorry, spectacle. Some have pouted because they failed to get a call to a certain church, or because they were not elected to membership on some board, or appointed to a certain committee, or elected to a certain office, or chosen to preach a Convention sermon. Some have pouted because they have gone down in defeat after trying their best to win a victory for Christ. But here is an unusual story of a man who pouted because he had won a victory. He was mad when he should have been glad. He retired. He did not retire because he reached the "age limit," nor because he was "resigned" by his church, nor because he wanted to boast of a victory which he thought justified his retirement. He retired because he thought he was discredited by the non-fulfillment of his prophecy. He thought more of his reputation as a prophet than he thought of the welfare of the people of a great city—and he has successors even to this day. Although God had greatly taught him, marvelously blessed and spared him, and wonderfully used him, yet he made of fellowship. If God gives us a second chance it will only be a later chapter of his amazing grace to perverse preachers. If we are so singularly blessed as to have a great revival, we have only to remember that Jonah had a record-breaking revival which was not brought to pass by extensive preliminary work with placards and newspaper publicity and dozens of committees and an hundred other human devices. If we feel the need of some such crutches to help us do our campaigning, Jonah reminds us that he got by without such things. If we lack faith as we go afield, we are rebuked by this man of faith who knew before he went to Nineveh that the message he was commanded to speak would turn the city right side up. Indeed, this was his excuse for not going the first time. If the revival does not end to our liking we can make us a booth and wait for the gourd, the worm, and the wind.

A Popular Preacher

It can hardly be thought an injustice to Jonah to classify him as a popular preacher. His ministry was two-fold. His first work was to stimulate the king of the Northern Kingdom to the religious reform of the Ten Tribes. His other and later task was to preach to Nineveh. He seems to have had a good home and to have been held in high esteem by his people. He undoubtedly had a successful ministry there. He may not have had an enemy in all the land. Alas, such pastorates do not last very long and one may seriously doubt if they are often very successful. Woe unto the preacher of whom every one speaks well. You hear very little about Jonah's life and work in this field but a whole book is given to the other part of his life work. When a man goes down into Gethsemane and finds God's plan for his life and comes out determined to fit his life into the groove of God's plan, there will soon be enough happening in the life and ministry of that man to fill a book. There isn't much worth the writing about a man until he passes this place. This was true in the case of Jonah, and this fact would not only entitle him to a seat on the platform at a preachers' convention but to a place on the program. Many have been placed on the program for much less than this.

But there is another thing which puts Jonah in the list of popular preachers and that is the fact that he preferred to run away rather than to preach what was given unto him. This is a plank of first magnitude in the platform of popular preachers. It didn't fit any better in the platform of Jonah than it does in other platforms now. Jonah's plan miscarried and he did something that many popular preachers have not done—he admitted that he was to blame for the storm. One could wish that some of his successors might be given grace enough to do this today. After a committee waited on Jonah he was picked up by a submarine which was bound in the direction of Nineveh. Jonah's brief day as a popular minister ended when God ordered him to Nineveh a second time; it was already history when the whale let down the gang plank for him to go ashore. For three days preceding his landing he was as uncomfortable as any other popular preacher on an old-fashioned mourner's bench. Some men with less experience than this have been elected president of the preachers' convention.

The world has far too few weeping prophets of God. Paul ceased not by the space of three years to warn the people of Ephesus night and day with tears. He did not succeed very well as a popular preacher in Athens, but he went to Corinth "in weakness and in fear, and in much trembling." He determined not to know anything among the Corinthians save Christ and Him crucified, and his speech and his preaching was not with enticing words of man's wisdom. The result was that the faith of his converts did not stand in the wisdom of men but in the power of God. God calls men and gives them their messages. They are to "preach the preaching" that He bids them. He sent Paul into Arabia for the space of three years to get a message that would transform the world, and he sent Jonah down into the deep, even to the bottom of the mountains, to learn his lesson and get his message. Paul came back from Arabia preaching Christ as the only hope of mankind. When Jonah got out of school he preached one sermon which shook the foundations of the city of Nineveh and put approximately a million people into sackcloth and ashes. Men who have had far less success have been given an honorary degree and were re-elected president of the preachers' convention.

A Praying Preacher

Dr. Gambrell once said: "Every once in a while every preacher ought to set himself out in front of himself and ask himself some questions." He also said: "No man is going to earn his salt as a preacher if he can't see higher than circumstances and conditions." This is sane philosophy. A preacher will never see higher than circumstances and conditions until he prays through. A preacher is engaged in a healthful exercise when he sets himself out in front of himself for a rigid examination as to his prayer life, for upon this everything else depends. Words cannot be found to set forth how immeasurably important it is that Christ's ambassadors should pray. It is doubtful if any church can be found whose spiritual current is deeper than the prayer life of its pastor. There is a very close relation between the prayer service of Jonah in the sea and the genuine repentance of the people of Nineveh a little later.

Jonah prayed. Things begin to happen when a man prays.

himself a booth outside the city and became more concerned about gourds than he was about the salvation of souls—and in this he has far too many followers even today.

Jonah's anger over God's mercy is amazing. He forgot that the highest function of preaching is to bear the message of divine mercy to all classes. This heathen city was a menace to Israel and Jonah really wanted it destroyed. He knew before he went to Nineveh that the message of God would turn the city. Some preachers have gone forth to preach with a fear of failure, but Jonah went to Nineveh with a fear of success. That which he feared came to pass. He was not disappointed. He expected God to show mercy. He was angry because mercy was shown.

God's mercy to Nineveh is a marvelous display of divine goodness. It was shown because of the change in the people of that city. They were in the path of God's wrath. When they repented, they came over into the path of God's mercy, and God spared them. God's attitude toward them corresponded to their response to His message. Jonah was honored of the Lord to be allowed to bear that message. God's aim in sending Jonah was the repentance of Nineveh to the end that He might bless it. Jonah should have been the first to rejoice over God's mercy to Nineveh.

The word *unusual* is overworked now-a-days, but it is about the best word to use in discussing Jonah. He was an unusual man, with an unusual experience with God, an unusual opportunity, an unusual success, many unusual tokens of divine favor, and yet he climaxed it all with an unusual attitude toward an unusual success. God was good to him, and so we leave him in his booth, outside the city, pouting and learning another lesson from God. It is worthy of notice that the Book of Jonah closes with God speaking the last word. God always has the last word. Jonah probably learned that it is much better to let God have the first word, the last word, and every other word about His plans for lost men, and for his own poor life. At least, preachers can learn many lessons from Jonah.

BORN TO PREACH

BORN TO PREACH

BORN TO PREACH